U MAD?

U can stop being angry at God,
others, and yourself once and for all.

DR. DIMITRI BRADLEY

Praise for *U Mad?*

"Anger may be the dominant driving force in our culture today. There's plenty to be angry about, but when anger starts controlling us, it ends up destroying our potential and our future. That's why Dr. Dimitri Bradley's new book *U Mad?* is so important right now. It will show you how to understand your anger, move beyond it, and channel your emotion in a positive way. Get this book and buy one for a friend. Each of us needs it, our community needs it, and this country definitely needs it."

—Phil Cooke, media consultant, filmmaker, and author of *One Big Thing: Discovering What You Were Born to Do.*

"I'm 'mad' about this book; it's that good. *U Mad?* spoke to me. It addressed some things I know I can do better and at the same time encouraged me with practical ideas for lifelong change. Get ready to get better. Peace is coming to your life. It's time to get rid of the daily drag of anger."

—John Mason, author of numerous best-selling books, including *An Enemy Called Average.*

"When it comes to navigating the minefield of our personal emotions, I have found that most believers take one of two approaches. The first approach is to 'over-spiritualize' the situation and therefore often never really get to the root of the issue. The second approach is to treat our emotional lives like a 'bad neighborhood'— we just refuse to go in at all (and especially not alone!).

I think all of us have at times done one or the other, without great success. That's why I am grateful for, and excited to recommend, the book that you now hold.

Dr. Dimitri Bradley has written a spiritually insightful, yet practical book, to help you and me recognize, accept, and confront the emotion of anger and overcome it! Drawing from his own experience and personal reflection, he helps us—with humor and without condemnation—to move past denial and embarrassment and deal with the issue of anger authentically and boldly with the power of God's Word.

I highly recommend this work, whether you have recognized that you are dealing with anger issues yourself, or desire to lovingly understand and assist someone else through this journey. Dr. Bradley, with this book, has helped us all!"

—Bishop Clarence E. McClendon, Ph.D., D.D.
Pastor of "The Place of Grace" and founder
of Clarence E. McClendon Ministries.

"Have you noticed that the world seems to be getting angrier? Everything from the personal to the political, to race relations and road rage is tainted by anger. I am so glad Dr. Dimitri Bradley has written a book that will go a long way in bringing much-needed help and solutions. Read it...then order one for someone who's mad."

—Bishop Michael Pitts, Cornerstone Global Network.

"Dr. Dimitri Bradley has done it again! He is wise enough and bold enough to deal with issues of life that may hold us back. His book, *U Mad?* is a must read for anyone who wants to go from recovery to discovery in their life."

—Tim Storey, Life Coach.

Dedication

I would like to dedicate this book to my wife, Nicole, and our children, Jordan and Julius. Your support in all of my endeavors has been extremely important and valuable to me over the years.

Contents

Acknowledgements...9

Introduction...11

Chapter 1: My Anger Journey.......................................13

Chapter 2: You Might Need Anger Management If….......23

Chapter 3: Fact Check..35

Chapter 4: Why Are You Angry?...................................45

Chapter 5: What Type of Angry Are You?
Passive or Judgmental...55

Chapter 6: What Type of Angry Are You?
Overwhelmed or Aggressive...65

Chapter 7: The Price of Anger.......................................77

Chapter 8: The Anger Action Step.................................87

Chapter 9: The Practice of Forgiveness..........................97

Chapter 10: The Principle of Thankfulness....................109

Chapter 11: More Practical Steps to Dealing with Anger....121

Chapter 12: Vain Imagination..129

Chapter 13: Pride: The Precursor to Anger.....................141

Chapter 14: Blessed Are the Peacemakers.......................153

Acknowledgements

First, I would like to thank my Heavenly Father, my Savior and Lord Jesus Christ, who alone enlightened and revealed to me the truth on how to overcome my anger.

I want to thank my church family and the viewers of our broadcast, who have supported me and this ministry over the last eighteen years.

A book like this takes a team effort, and I would like to acknowledge and thank those who helped make it happen. It is not my desire to leave anyone out, so if I fail to mention your name, it was not my intent. A sincere thank you goes out to every person who played a part in making this book a reality.

Thank you to all of the great men of God who I learned from and inspired me over the years. Special thanks to Ron Carpenter who introduced me to Phil Cooke, who in turn connected me with John Mason, who played a major role in bringing this book to fruition. I want to thank Cameron Hardison who took the time to read some of my material and critique some of my first attempts. And I want to thank my staff for taking care of the day-to-day operations so I could focus on accomplishing this important task.

Blessings to you all!

Introduction

Are you angry?

There's a lot to be angry about in our world. We get fresh reports of injustice, tragedy, and offenses daily. It seems like all you have to do is take one look at the news to see a new reason to be sad, disappointed, and, yes, angry.

I wrote this book from a place that I occupied. That is to say, I have been an angry man. And I have seen many other people who are dealing with anger, just as I have, all around me. I knew I must minister about the topic of anger because it is a place where I needed healing in my own life.

As an African-American pastor living today in the United States, I see things through different eyes than some people. While I didn't grow up in the ghetto, it was about one block over, and I have seen all kinds of reasons people from that background are angry. But I didn't stay there; in fact, I became very successful, so I have seen the reasons why people from other backgrounds are also angry.

Growing up, I tried to manage my anger with things like sports. Frankly, football is therapeutic for me, and I see a great deal of myself in my own son who, even though he has grown up with a very different life than I had, has a "switch." Those of us tapping anger in athletics can sometimes use that anger to try to harder. Sports often offer an outlet for young men to vent the anger that is bubbling up inside them, but this is one of just many ways we try to handle the anger that is sometimes simmering just beneath the surface.

But anger is not a young man's issue. Anger is not a black issue. It is not a white issue. It is not a male issue or female issue. It is not just an issue for the poor, or for the rich. It is a prevalent problem for people of every race, gender, socioeconomic status, and even faith.

Being a Christian does not mean that you will never have anger issues. It may mean that you try to hide and stuff them deep down, but simply having faith is not in and of itself the sole solution for how we handle anger.

The good thing is that God understands our frame (see Psalm 103:14). That means that because He is the One who made us, He understands all our frailties, weaknesses, and needs—physical, spiritual, and emotional. He is not surprised that we deal with anger problems, but you may be surprised to learn that we are capable of anger because God is! We are made in His likeness, capable of passionate emotions like love and tenderness...but also anger.

However, it is not His intention that we let the emotions He gave us, such as anger, control us. God gave us minds we can use to make good choices or bad ones, and He gave us a spirit that can be redeemed through knowing Jesus Christ. He designed our redeemed spirits to be in the drivers' seats of our lives, and sometimes to do so we must bump emotions like our anger out of the leading position they have occupied.

We must be willing to let God do work behind the scenes on the things we keep hidden, such as our anger. The amazing thing few realize is that when we replace anger and pride with His way of doing things, we can receive some truly life-changing promises from God! I want to tell you about those promises and offer you an alternative to living an angry life—even for those of you who don't realize you are dealing with anger.

If you would like to replace your anger and all the consequences and side effects that come with it and exchange them for the gifts and blessings of God, I invite you to join me on a journey beyond anger management and learn how to bring this powerful emotion into subjection under God and His Word.

1
MY ANGER JOURNEY

I became truly aware of my own anger one day on the way to church. As my family and I were leaving the house on our way to the service, one of my neighbors stepped out in front of my car and refused to get out of the way when he saw we were coming. He was busy doing his thing, and he seemed to have a real attitude about it— throwing up some dirty looks at us. He seemed perfectly content to take his time instead of just moving out of the way briefly so we could go by. I found it offensive to be disrespected like this.

Remember, I'm on my way to church; but I got out of the car to confront the guy. My wife, Nicole said, "You can't be doing this! I can't believe you're doing this...." But I ignored her.

"Hey, what are you doing?" I demanded as I walked toward him. I could feel the heat building within me, and I just wanted to slug this guy and be done with it.

As I walked toward him, I recognized within myself that I was in real danger of losing it. It was almost like an out-of-body experience, because I suddenly saw myself with an observer's perspective.

Mid-conversation, I literally stopped myself, turned around, and got back in the car. I was thinking, "That was about the stupidest thing I could've done." He could've had a knife or a gun, could've started to escalate a confrontation, might've been crazy or on drugs...

And those aren't even counting the things *I* may have done! What if I had taken a swing at him, starting a fight? What if he brought me up on assault charges because I was the one who initiated a fight by getting out of the car and losing my cool?

The thing that scared me most was that I had been on a razor's edge of losing control with this guy and possibly even hurting him...

...on the way to *preach* at church!

Yes, that's right, this wasn't right after I was saved. The *pastor* almost started a fight with a guy who simply didn't get out of the way fast enough while I was trying to get to church to preach God's Word. I could just picture the news headline: *"Pastor Assaults Neighbor on Way to Preach Sermon."*

I saw clearly that I *definitely* had an anger issue.

The question was, if being saved and even being a preacher wasn't enough to fix the problem, what was? I determined to seek the Lord and find out.

Childhood Anger

Although I grew up in a two-parent household, the neighborhood could test you physically more often than you might expect. I had to learn to handle myself. My father played a big role in my life, and he made it clear we were not to start fights but we should end them when necessary. I believe his intention was for us to know how to survive in a tough environment. By the time I came along, my dad was pretty laid back, but my mom told me that he used to be a tough customer. He was from Philadelphia, and I've heard some stories about how he used to carry a gun and wasn't to be trifled with. I never saw that part of my dad, but he did teach me that we would not get rolled over. He knew we needed to be able to fight, but he tried to make sure we knew when it was appropriate. He taught us the rules.

We seem more aware of bullying now than when I was a child, but it is nothing new. Fighting was a pretty typical part of living in a tough area, and if you couldn't defend yourself, they were going to take advantage of you. Somewhere along the line, I discovered that I did a whole lot better at defending myself when I was *mad*.

By nature, I'm a pretty laid back person. I don't start fights. However, while growing up I would sometimes just snap in a confrontation. I noticed that people were actually afraid of me when this would happen, so at some level of consciousness I knew that if I wanted people to leave me alone and not bully me, I had to hit "the switch."

One time while I was a kid in elementary school, this older kid across the street pushed me too far. We used to play together when we were younger, but as we got older we fought—and since I was smaller and younger, I didn't get to do a whole lot of fighting back because it was so uneven. Mostly, I just took abuse. But one day, he pushed me so far, I went back to my house and grabbed a steak knife! Luckily, my father caught me.

"What you going to do?" he asked. I didn't have a good explanation because I hadn't really thought it through, so he said, "No, you are not doing this. This is not how we do it. If you need to, go back and fight him, but not with this." If my dad hadn't intervened, I likely would've walked back out there and would've tried to stab that other boy because I was so mad and frustrated. I now see I already had an anger problem.

I remember another time when we were playing catch with a football before class in the schoolyard. I was just starting middle school. This big kid walked up, and while I didn't know him, everyone else seemed to—and was afraid of him. He took our ball and stopped the game. No one else said anything, but I asked him, "Why are you doing this? What's the big deal?"

He was not going to just take my ball from me! So, I took the ball back. A full-fledged fight ensued, and even though this was one of the bigger, tougher guys at my new middle school, we quickly found out I was tougher! (He actually became my friend later, but that's beside the point.)

In middle school we had to take an elective, and I selected band. I will never forget that one time the kid sitting next to me just wouldn't stop teasing me. He kept at it, and when I told him to stop, he would not leave me alone. I did everything I knew to do to get him to leave me alone. I knew it wouldn't do any good to tell the teacher because even if you did, the teachers didn't do anything to stop it.

I had broken my finger from playing football, but that didn't stop me—this kid pushed me too far, and I just snapped! I went off on him, and I'm not trying to brag by saying that I wailed on him with one hand, but it shows how far I had let my anger go even by that point. They had to pull me off him.

My fellow classmates were very surprised, because they had never seen that part of me. But I had; in fact, I had cultivated and used that anger as a survival tool.

What I didn't know was that instead of me having a handle on it, it was handling me.

I had done everything I knew to do to stop that kid, but it seemed yet again the only solution was to let go of the leash I kept on the beast of my anger. However, as I grew up, that leash became increasingly frayed and hard to hold onto. The "switch" had a hair trigger.

My environment told me that there was respect and peace to be found if I would use my anger to fight and *take* that respect. All I had to do was flip the switch.

Nobody told me that it would backfire on me later in life.

As I grew older, the fights became less frequent—but the stakes were higher. People started carrying weapons, and fights wouldn't just mean a bloody nose. They could mean blood on the floor—mine!

My anger went underground. I had given it a place in my life, trying to harness its power, and while the expression of my anger wasn't so obvious, it was crouching behind the scenes, waiting to get out. I let it out on the football field, and sometimes it showed around the edges, but it became a subtler thing and harder to point out as being a problem.

Let God Show You What's Wrong

The interesting thing is that before that day on the way to church where I almost slugged my neighbor, if you had asked me if I had an anger issue, I likely would've told you no. It has surprised me to learn that many of the people who harbor anger in their lives don't even recognize that they have a problem in this area.

In fact, you may be reading this book right now because someone gave it to you, and you may not even realize that you have a problem with anger. I didn't, and it took a (blessedly uneventful) wake-up call for me to recognize that I needed to give God some space to work on this.

As I began to pray, the Lord started to show me, even through my interactions with my family, that I really did have a problem with anger. Before coming to this realization, I would've shot down any notion that I needed help dealing with it.

But you can't get better if you don't know what's wrong.

I would go so far as to say that I think most people with anger problems don't know that they are angry. Anger comes in many forms and takes many different shapes. It is different for men and women, old and young. For men, anger can be more obvious—we often get loud or even violent, manifesting our anger externally. Women display it differently, and it is more common for them to internalize their anger, though we're all familiar with the loud, angry woman stereotype.

Different types of people display anger in different ways, which we will get into later in the book. But right now I want you to know you are not alone, and no one is pointing fingers or blame at you.

In fact, if you deal with anger issues, you are in good company.

God Uses Angry People

It may surprise you to learn that some famous people, people we think of as being "good people," got angry. Many of us who follow sports are aware of the former running back from the Baltimore Ravens who struck his girlfriend in the elevator. If he knew what that angry outburst would cost him, he may have worked on getting it under control earlier. But I'm not talking about the latest angry athlete; I'm talking about the people in the Bible.

Many people, including most Christians, don't think about Moses as having an anger problem. However, a quick look at his life's lowest points shows that this incredible man of God got into some serious trouble when he gave place to his anger.

Moses, who grew up as part of Pharaoh's household, eventually learned that he was a Hebrew. Some Bible scholars believe that at some point before God spoke to him from the burning bush Moses may have gotten it into his head that he would be a savior for his people.

One day he came across an Egyptian slave master abusing one of the Hebrew slaves. We read, *"So he looked this way and that way, and when he saw no one, he killed the Egyptian and hid him in the sand"* (Exodus 2:12). While this was probably a crime of passion and idealism, the fact that Moses looked around first to see if anyone was looking tells us he knew what he was doing was wrong. Nevertheless, he gave place to his anger, and he murdered the Egyptian.

Later, he came across two Hebrews fighting, and his prideful opinion of himself led him to try to settle the argument. The slave who was hitting the other slave replied, "*Who made you a prince and a judge over us? Do you intend to kill me as you killed the Egyptian?*" (Exodus 2:14)

Perhaps Moses tried to let his anger make him a savior for his people, but now instead of being known as a savior, he was known as a dangerous hothead—a *murderer*!

And this was not the only time Moses' anger got the better of him. When he learned that others knew he had murdered the Egyptian, Moses fled into the desert. There he lived for forty years, tending sheep. You may not know this, but sheep are *dumb*, so tending sheep was either going to pacify Moses or continue to give him a reason to be angry. Maybe it was some of both, but at least forty years after killing the Egyptian, Moses' anger got him in trouble again.

Many who are not even Christians are familiar with the Ten Commandments. Moses went up onto a mountain for forty days to commune with God, and God gave him the ten fundamental laws He wanted His people to live by. These rules are the foundation for law and government in every Western nation, a heritage of our Judeo-Christian roots. They fall into two categories: our relationship with God, and our relationship with each other. "Do not murder" is a pretty important rule, and the fact that God could use Moses—even though he had disobeyed this cardinal commandment about how we interact with others—says a lot about how merciful God is.

So, Moses had been gone a long time—forty days up on the mountain. In his absence, the people had gone *wild*. Thinking Moses dead, they took gold they had received from the Egyptians and formed it into a golden calf to worship. What's more, as Moses came down the mountain, he saw they were having a giant party. This was not a common Jewish party with dancing and matzo balls; it was likely more like a hedonistic drunken orgy.

When Moses saw this, again his anger issue came to the surface. We read, "*So it was, as soon as he came near the camp, that he saw the calf and the dancing. So Moses' anger became hot, and he cast the tablets out of his hands and broke them at the foot of the mountain"* (Exodus 32:19).

Moses was so mad that he took the words God chiseled onto stone tablets, the results of forty days of communion with the Lord, and smashed them! You might think that after spending all that time with God, Moses wouldn't be likely to have such a fleshly reaction as a bout of anger like this. But he did, and that was not the last time.

When frustrated by the complaining children of Israel as they wandered in the desert, Moses reverted to his old ways by striking a rock. This doesn't sound so bad, and in fact God had told him to strike a rock on a previous occasion and water flowed from it. This time, Moses hit the rock twice, and water still gushed out, but there was a problem.

First, Moses seems to have hit the rock twice out of anger and frustration. Second, and more importantly, God had told him to *speak* to the rock. He wasn't supposed to do things as he had done them before; God was showing Moses a new way. But Moses, in his frustration, struck out instead, and this was actually a significant problem between him and God.

I tell you all this about Moses because to the Hebrew people, Moses is completely revered. Moses gave them God's law, the system Jews live by till this day. Moses was also the one who recorded the opening five books of the Bible, called the Torah, Psalm 90, and possibly even the book of Job. Everything that made Judaism truly Judaism came from God through this man Moses.

Yet as God greatly used him, at times Moses had trouble dealing with his anger. There are even other times I didn't mention that paint a picture of Moses with a temper.

I tell you all this to illustrate that you are not alone in dealing with your anger, and even good men and women who are used by God can wrestle with this issue. It does not disqualify you from service to God or from being a good Christian, and it is not something shameful for you to hide.

But that does not mean that God does not want to work with you on it. He loves us as we are, but He loves us too much to leave us as He finds us. If you will let Him, God will not leave your anger problem alone—He will heal you.

Moses died at a very old age. And, interestingly, he became known as the humblest man who ever lived. This is a topic we will revisit later in the book, because pride and anger have a very strong connection. If Moses could start his life known as a murderer and a person who vented his anger by killing the Egyptian, shattering the Ten Commandments, and striking rock and yet end his life known as the most humble man who ever lived, it should give you great hope!

God used him despite his anger, and He will use you, too.

Jesus Got Angry...and Did Not Sin

Moses is not the only angry person in the Bible. Plenty of others struggled with their anger as well, but possibly more surprising is that Jesus Himself sometimes displayed anger.

We read that Jesus was deeply distressed when Lazarus died. It says, "*When Jesus saw her weeping and saw the other people wailing with her, a deep anger welled up within him, and he was deeply troubled. 'Where have you put him?' he asked them. They told him, 'Lord, come and see.' Then Jesus wept. The people who were standing nearby said, 'See how much he loved him!'*" (John 11:33-36 NLT)

Right after Jesus entered Jerusalem, on His path to His crucifixion and resurrection, He entered the temple and drove out the people doing business there *with a whip.*

We read, "*Jesus entered the Temple and began to drive out all the people buying and selling animals for sacrifice. He knocked over the tables of the money changers and the chairs of those selling doves. He said to them, 'The Scriptures declare, "My Temple will be called a house of prayer," but you have turned it into a den of thieves!'"* (Matthew 21:12-13 NLT)

This does not exactly fit our mold of the soft and passive Jesus; this is Jesus with fire in Him! This is Jesus righteously angry at sickness, pain, and injustice.

It leads to a very interesting question: If Jesus did it, is it wrong to be angry?

We find a potentially perplexing answer that we will explore at length in this book. Psalm 4:4 says, *"Be angry, and do not sin...."* Another translation says, *"Don't sin by letting anger control you..."* (NLT). In Ephesians 4:26-27, the Apostle Paul quotes this verse when he is talking about putting off our old failings and putting on our new Christian nature. He says, *"'Be angry, and do not sin'; do not let the sun go down on your wrath, nor give place to the devil."*

I believe we can draw a conclusion from this. I can tell you with confidence that simply being angry *is not a sin*. There is a difference between experiencing the emotion of anger, even letting it motivate us in certain settings, and sinning by *letting it control us*, which gives the devil a foothold in our lives.

God began to show me the difference between the healthy emotion He created us with and the sin of letting anger control me as I approached Him in prayer. It is my prayer now that as we explore this issue together, you too can uncover your own anger issues and learn to deal with them *God's* way. This is not "anger management" the way the world sees it. This is handling our anger with the tools that God has provided, and they are powerful tools that will lead to your freedom in this area!

If you want to experience the freedom and blessing of God and resolve any anger issues, whether they are hidden or obvious, join me in looking at some signs you may be dealing with an anger problem. It is very likely you will see yourself in the following pages, but the sooner you accept this is a problem for you, the sooner you can begin to experience lasting freedom.

2

YOU MIGHT NEED ANGER MANAGEMENT IF...

In the previous chapter, I mentioned that there have been a lot of angry people in the Bible. As I prayed about my own anger issues, God used some of these stories to teach me things about our anger that I want to share with you. I want to help you identify yourself, to see yourself in some of these stories, and to become aware of the anger that may be running like an undercurrent that is poisoning your life and robbing you of peace and joy.

The first angry person we find in the Bible shows up early— chapter 4 of Genesis. In fact, the dysfunctional story of the first family gives us the first angry person letting his anger take the driver's seat in his life, with tragic consequences.

Adam and Eve had two sons—Cain and Abel, who you've likely heard about. Abel grew up to be a shepherd, but Cain was a farmer. We read that in the process of time (Cain's real problem), he *"presented some of his crops as a gift to the Lord. Abel also brought a gift—the best of the firstborn lambs from his flock. The Lord accepted Abel and his gift, but he did not accept Cain and his gift. This made Cain very angry, and he looked dejected"* (Genesis 4:3-5 NLT).

It is important to understand that while it looks like they did the same thing, they did not. They both brought offerings, but Abel brought the correct kind of sacrifice Adam would have taught them to offer—the first and the best. Cain brought whatever he brought when it seemed good to him to bring it, and this is why God did not accept Cain's offering.

It may have gone like this: They both put their offerings on the altar, and when they came back in the morning Abel's offering had been consumed by fire and Cain's was still there, unaccepted. God rejected it. Cain did not get the results he wanted or that his brother got.

God gives Cain some of the best instruction about anger and sin in the whole Bible. "*'Why are you so angry?' the Lord asked Cain. 'Why do you look so dejected? You will be accepted if you do what is right. But if you refuse to do what is right, then watch out! Sin is crouching at the door, eager to control you. But you must subdue it and be its master'*" (Genesis 4:6-7 NLT). When we do not do what is right, we give an opening to sin. Instead of letting it control us, by the power of the Holy Spirit, we must conquer it. This definitely includes anger.

We next read that the very first family was likely more dysfunctional than yours, unless you are killing one another. It says in Genesis 4:8, "*Now Cain talked with Abel his brother; and it came to pass, when they were in the field, that Cain rose up against Abel his brother and killed him.*"

Displaced Anger

Here is what I want you to see about this: Cain was not actually angry with Abel. Cain's issue wasn't with his brother; it was with *God*. But Cain did not take his issue up with the person he's angry with; he took it out on someone else.

One of the signs that your anger is out of control is when you tend to take it out on people other than the source of where it came from. This is called displaced anger, and we've all been guilty of this at one time or another. However, if this is your habit, you may need God's style of anger management.

We're all familiar with displaced anger—the harmony of our house is destroyed when we get home and explode on everybody because we've had a bad day. The problem happened at work, but we bring it home with us. We can't yell at our boss, so we take it out on our spouse, or our kids, or even the dog.

Now, while this happens to everyone from time to time, it is a problem if the people in your family can see this coming—they're used to it, and they're all watching carefully to see if you are in a mood when you walk in the door. If everyone is laughing and joking and having fun and they all stop when you come home, and you *haven't even said anything yet*, you may have an anger problem.

When we displace our anger like this, we're taking it out on the wrong people. Cain could have brought his anger to God in prayer, and while he could not act out inappropriately against God like he did with Abel, he could've dealt with his anger by addressing the One he was angry with. Instead, he turned on an innocent person, his brother.

If you take your anger out on the innocent people around you instead of dealing with your problem and the source of your anger, not only is it injustice to them, it will not even actually help with the underlying source of your anger. It won't help! It may blow off steam for a moment, but the underlying source of your anger will not improve or get better when you choose to give place to your anger in this fashion. You are not just hurting those around you; you are hurting yourself, too.

This kind of anger is a sin. It is a sin against those you are attacking. Even if you are not striking and killing them, Jesus tells us, "*But I say to you that whoever is angry with his brother without a cause shall be in danger of the judgment. And whoever says to his brother,*

'Raca!' shall be in danger of the council. But whoever says, 'You fool!' shall be in danger of hell fire" (Matthew 5:22).

Displacing your anger is serious, and if you are doing it routinely as a way of trying to manage your anger, you've got an anger problem, and you need God's help to deal with it. The good news is that you can *"subdue it and be its master,"* and you can conquer this inappropriate way of dealing with your anger—even if you are angry with God.

Angry When You Don't Get Your Way

The next angry person from the Bible I want to talk about is Jonah. The T. D. Jakes of his generation, Jonah, was the premier prophet of his time. God gave him some instructions: He was to go to Israel's enemy, Nineveh, and preach to them that if they did not repent, God was going to destroy the city.

The thing is, Jonah *wanted* God to destroy them. Jonah was angry with the Ninevites and wanted them wiped out; he didn't want them to repent and turn from their sins so God would spare them.

So he ran. Instead of going to Nineveh, he headed to Tarshish. If you've ever been in Sunday school, you likely know how he was in a terrible storm while running from God, only to be swallowed by a giant fish or whale! In the belly of the beast, Jonah repents of disobeying God by running, but he really hasn't changed his heart about Nineveh. When he's vomited up on the beach, he obeys and preaches the message of judgment and repentance God gave him, but there was a problem: He knew that when he preached God's messages, people repented. He still didn't want that.

When God saw that the people are genuinely repentant, He changed His mind and does not destroy the city. This was *exactly* why Jonah ran in the first place—the Word of God brings people to repentance. Even evil Ninevites!

We read, "*But it displeased Jonah exceedingly, and he became angry*" (Jonah 4:1). In fact, it bothered him so much, he asked God to just *kill him*!

"*Then the Lord said, 'Is it right for you to be angry?'*" (Jonah 4:4).

So, I ask you this: With whom was Jonah angry? The people for listening to his message and repenting? I don't think so. I think Jonah was angry with *God*. He was angry with God because he didn't get his way, and these people he didn't like were not destroyed because God did exactly what He said He'd do—spare them if they repented.

You need anger management if you are mad with God because things did not turn out the way you wanted them to.

We all get angry with God occasionally—or sad or disappointed. But when you don't get your way, do you regularly find yourself ticked off at God? Do you find yourself *still* angry with God over things that happened months, years, even *decades* ago? If so, you probably have an anger problem.

As is the case with nearly all angry outbursts, there is always more to the story than we see and understand. One technique I will give you when dealing with your anger is to stop and get the facts, and I promise you this: You never, ever have all the facts when it comes to the things for which you are angry with God. You do not know all He knows, and you do not see all He sees. If you are angry about something, it is because you do not understand the whole picture like He does, and there is a great deal going on behind the scenes you may not know about until you can ask Him in eternity.

Get the Rest of the Story

I have experienced these confusing circumstances where many times I didn't see the whole picture. A story that comes to mind was when I was a young, up-and-coming member of the banking community. I had been on the job perhaps six or eight months, and I was really excelling at certain things that were getting recognized. I was the new guy, but my hard work was getting noticed. I thought I was on the fast track to promotion and advancement.

That's why it was a total shock when, as the low man on the totem pole, I learned that I would be let go! I couldn't believe it. My numbers were excellent, and I was outperforming many of the people who had been there far longer than I had been. Why not let one of them go, I wondered.

Honestly, it made me angry. I had worked very hard to show them what kind of person I was and what I was capable of and committed to doing. I felt like all my hard work was going unrecognized and unrewarded. Where was the blessing and favor of God?

I didn't know the whole story. There were things going on behind the scenes I would learn shortly that would diffuse my anger.

The owner of the company called me soon after I was let go. He told me about some things that were happening in the company and changes coming down the pike. "I want you to come back" after it is over, he told me. "And we're not going to change your salary—you will come back and do your old job." The company was going through restructuring, and I wasn't the only person who was going to be let go—they were cleaning house and laying off the whole department. I was just the first, but unlike many of the others, they wanted me back when the dust cleared. In fact, by letting me go the way they did, they preserved my ability to come back!

I didn't understand what was going on behind the scenes, because I didn't know everything the owner did. He had a plan for me, a way of working it out, and this is much like God. He has good plans for us, and while we may not understand all that is going on around us, He is working everything out for our good.

Romans 8:28 tells us, *"And we know that all things work together for good to those who love God, to those who are the called according to His purpose."*

What the devil intends for evil, God can work for our good. The best example of this is Joseph, who was sold into slavery by his own brothers. He ends up a slave in Egypt, but God was with him, and he excelled at everything he put his hand to. God blessed him and was with him...even when more bad things happened.

Thrown into prison for a crime he didn't commit, he again found favor, and more importantly, he was positioned to change the world and preserve God's people when he was called out of prison to interpret Pharaoh's dream. Because Joseph was in Egypt, doing his best with the difficult circumstances he encountered, he was exactly where he needed to be to rise to become the second most powerful man in Egypt. Because of his godly wisdom and leadership, Egypt stockpiled food and preserved countless lives through the coming famine.

Many years had passed when he saw his brothers again, yet while they feared him when they learned who he was, the anger Joseph no doubt felt toward them had lost its power over him. He had already used the key of forgiveness to break its hold. He was able to tell them, *"You intended to harm me, but God intended it all for good. He brought me to this position so I could save the lives of many people"* (Genesis 50:20 NLT).

Angry with God

People are angry for many reasons, but I have met many who are angry, underneath it all, with God. They did not get their way, or they think He wronged them; and while they may not even admit it to themselves, they're angry with God.

Preachers have often not made this any better. We unthinkingly say things such as, "God needed them in heaven," or "God took them" while preaching a funeral. When someone's heart is breaking after losing a loved one and we say some platitude like this, we cast God in a negative light. What young child or grieving widow wants to serve a God who would just up and take their loved one?

Insurance companies may label natural disasters "acts of God," and again we're feeding a lie that God isn't good and that He causes bad things to happen to people. I can understand why someone would be mad at God if they think He caused an earthquake or hurricane that destroyed their home or killed people. What kind of God would that be?

Other times people cast God into a bad light through their actions. Unsaved people may wander into a church full of judgmental Christians who proceed to reject them because of their dress, their behaviors, their language, their race, or their economic status. People far from God who see Christians behave in this unloving manner are partly justified in thinking that if *these* folk represent God, they don't want anything to do with Him.

An abusive father may hurt a child, and when she grows up she cannot stomach the idea of God as a loving Father because her own idea of a father was poisoned growing up. Why would God let that happen to her? Why didn't He prevent it? How can she ever know Him as "Father" when that very word carries loathing and bitterness with it?

As long as we blame God for these things and get angry, we create a barrier to His peace and power in our lives.

We may think that these injustices wrongly blamed on God don't really mean anything, but they are part of the biggest lie told since the Garden of Eden: "God isn't all good, and He can't be completely trusted. Because someday, for some reason you can't understand, He's going to do something that may hurt you...and there's nothing you can do about it."

This is not the God of the Bible. This is not our loving Heavenly Father, and it is not the heart of God revealed in the actions and character of His Son, Jesus, who only did on the earth what He saw the Father do. Jesus made it clear that He came to earth to give us life as a free gift—abundant life.

The truth is, "*The thief does not come except to steal, and to kill, and to destroy. I* [Jesus] *have come that they may have life, and that they may have it more abundantly*" (John 10:10). God sent His only Son to earth to die for us because He loved us so much; it is the enemy who steals, kills, and destroys in this world. If we want to be angry with anyone, it is him! But he masterfully misdirects our anger away from himself and toward God.

Dear reader, God did not take your loved one. He did not send the hurricane, and small-minded, bitter people do not accurately represent Him (except that He loves them, too). He did not stand by uncaringly while you were hurt, and He is 100 percent good—all the time, every time, to everyone.

We wrongly hold God accountable for things He did not do. We live in a fallen world currently ruled by a bitter, cruel enemy in whom there is no goodness or truth. God is behind all goodness, and the enemy is behind every lie about God, just as he has been from the beginning in the Garden.

When we learn one of the greatest keys for dealing with anger, forgiveness (which I'll cover at length later in the book), then we can release the unforgiveness we have for God and, with it, our anger. As we will see, forgiveness is letting go of the offense we feel another has done against us...and finding that we have freed ourselves.

If anyone had a right to be angry with God, it was Joseph. For sharing with others the dreams God had given him, he was sold into slavery. In slavery, he was mistreated, falsely accused, and imprisoned. In prison, he was forgotten and languished in his confinement, no doubt thinking he'd never see the promise of those dreams come to pass.

Yet God's plan for Joseph's life *did* come to pass, and because he'd let go of his anger and bitterness, Joseph's heart was whole and healthy when he encountered his brothers again. Through this one man, who experienced what seemed to be so many injustices, God saved His people—and all of Egypt.

What have you been blaming God for doing? If He could work Joseph's circumstances for good, promoting Joseph and showing him favor, as well as preserving His people from a deadly famine, what could He be doing in your life? Is anything impossible for God?

Forgiveness is a powerful tool I cannot wait to explore with you in greater depth, but for now I want you to just open yourself to the possibility that any bad things you have been through are not God's fault. Consider that you have wrongly laid blame at His feet and that you have misplaced your anger, when in fact it is your enemy who has been conspiring against you.

It is time to not only forgive God, or others—it is time to ask for forgiveness. It is not uncommon to be angry with God; He's not going to strike you down with a lightning bolt! However, it is not for your good. It is keeping you in anger, and it is preventing you from fully experiencing His grace, peace, and power. Jesus tells us, "*Forgive, and you will be forgiven. Give, and it will be given to you: good measure, pressed down, shaken together, and running over will be put into your bosom. For with the same measure that you use, it will be measured back to you*" (Luke 6:37b-38). Isn't that how you'd like to receive from God—"*pressed down, shaken together, and running over*"?

Friend, in this book I will repeatedly urge you to forgive. Don't displace your anger onto the only One who is good; put the blame where it belongs, at the feet of the enemy of your soul. We live in a fallen world, and we have a very real enemy.

But the good news is that there is nothing he can do that God cannot work for your good! There is no pit too deep that God cannot pull you out. There is no prison so dark that He will forget you. There is no injustice that He will not redeem, restoring to you the years and good things your enemy has stolen.

However, you free up His flow of blessings by dealing with the anger and bitterness in your heart. The key to dealing with those things is simple: forgive. Let it go.

Then, stand back and watch as God redeems the years the locust has eaten (see Joel 2:25).

3
FACT CHECK

I have found that regardless of the type of anger that you have—which we will explore later in this book—or the trigger that sparks your anger, many people with anger issues have certain things in common. Perhaps the biggest one I have noticed is that anger thrives together with ignorance. The two feed off each other.

When we let ourselves fly off the handle and get angry, it is often because we lack important facts. If we truly understood what was going on, we oftentimes would not become so angry, but we are blinded by our own biases, expectations, emotional wounds, and judgments against ourselves, others, and God.

We had to have some roof work done on our church not long ago, and typically my staff takes care of things like this, but this day I just happened to walk through the lobby and this man started asking questions about the roof. In my mind I had already sized him up (he looked like he just walked off the set of Sons of Anarchy), and I wasn't feeling him at all. After talking with him just a few minutes, I discovered he was a solid Christian and was excited about working on the church. I was so wrong because I didn't have all the facts.

There's an interesting story in the Bible about someone who got angry before he had all the facts. An enemy of Israel once tried to pay a corrupt prophet to curse God's people, and on the way to do so, this prophet, Balaam, ran into problems. The donkey he was riding saw the angel of the Lord standing in the way with a drawn sword in his hand!

The donkey turned aside to avoid the angel, so Balaam struck the donkey to turn her back. The angel then stood in a narrow place between two vineyards, with a wall on either side, and when the donkey saw the angel again, she pushed herself against the wall, crushing Balaam's foot. So, he struck her again. Next, the angel of the Lord positioned himself in a narrow place where there was not room to go by either to the left or right, so when the donkey saw this, she lay down! We read that Balaam was so angry, he began to beat the donkey with his staff.

Now comes the interesting part: *"Then the Lord opened the mouth of the donkey, and she said to Balaam, 'What have I done to you, that you have struck me these three times?'"* (Numbers 22:28).

You know you have an anger problem when God has to make your donkey talk to you to get your attention!

"'You have made me look like a fool!' Balaam shouted. 'If I had a sword with me, I would kill you!'

"'But I am the same donkey you have ridden all your life,' the donkey answered. 'Have I ever done anything like this before?'

"'No,' Balaam admitted.

"Then the Lord opened Balaam's eyes, and he saw the angel of the Lord standing in the roadway with a drawn sword in his hand. Balaam bowed his head and fell face down on the ground before him" (Numbers 22:29-31 NLT).

Balaam did not have all the facts. If he did, he would have realized that the loyal animal he was beating had actually saved his life! The angel of the Lord then told him that if the donkey had not turned away, he certainly would have killed Balaam.

How often is this true for us—things don't go our way, so we fly off the handle, but we lack critical information? You may need anger management if you tend to get angry a lot, and later you learn that it was not justified because you did not have all the facts. If you often regret getting angry and have to apologize because you misunderstood something, took something wrong, or simply were ignorant when you went off, this may describe you.

When we have an anger problem, we allow our temper to get away from us so fast that we fly off the handle with other people without asking the right questions first. We can be very quick to get mad, and it can create quite a mess because we lack the necessary details. But while you can apologize for tearing up the room, your apology cannot put the room back together again. Our anger has lasting consequences.

I have found out that while you can apologize for the words you say, once they are out of your mouth, you cannot take them back. People can forgive you, but they cannot unhear what you've said.

It is better not to have said the angry things than it is to apologize for them.

Ask Questions

When we get angry quickly because things are not going the way we want or people are not doing what we want them to do, it can show that we are dealing with an underlying anger problem. Every human being is different, and we approach problems from different angles. We are not always going to get our own way, but when not getting our way or things happening differently than we'd planned makes us explode, we have anger issues to deal with.

Sometimes people are even acting in our best interests—even if they are not doing exactly what we told them to do, the way we told them to do it. They may be looking out for us, but because they aren't doing it the way we wanted, we might fly off the handle and beat them up with our words instead of asking them simple qualifying questions to find out what the story is. It is especially embarrassing to find out that what had made you so angry was actually happening for your *good*. Maybe someone was looking out for you or trying to keep you from a bigger problem, but because you did not know it, you blew up.

When we do this, it is because our anger is out of control. When you have an anger problem, you make a fuss first, and ask questions later...if at all.

But God has a better plan. *"A gentle answer turns away wrath, but a harsh word stirs up anger,"* we read in Proverbs 15:1 NIV.

Our angry words don't just stir up anger and others in turn, they can spread our tendency toward anger to our friends and loved ones. Proverbs 22:24–25 NIV says *"Do not make friends with a hot-tempered man, do not associate with one easily angered, or you may learn his ways and get yourself ensnared."*

When you are an angry tornado tearing through your house, you are sowing seeds...and will reap the whirlwind. You will gather a harvest you don't want from your spouse, and you are teaching a behavior to your children you never want to receive and that you will not want them to pass on to their spouses and children.

It is my goal to not just educate you about anger in this book; I want to help you get better. I want this to make your relationship with your spouse, your kids, your coworkers, and your friends better because you realize how much damage anger can do—to you and others. Harsh, angry, ignorant answers damage our relationships in lasting ways, and I believe God will show us a better way.

Instead of being quick to get angry, we should always ask questions first and reserve judgment until we've gathered all the facts. Then, sometimes it is justified to get angry, but many times it is not.

Asking questions before you let yourself be angry helps ensure that you don't have to apologize for embarrassing explosions. I have found we can prevent a lot of angry words by simply stopping to get the facts before we decide how to respond.

If you walk into the house to find a party going on, you may want to ask some questions—it might be a party for you! Or it could be because someone just got out of the hospital or landed their dream job. (On the other hand, it could be because your kids thought you were gone for the weekend and threw a party without your permission, in which case it is okay to get angry!)

Maybe you find out a coworker or subordinate did not do what you wanted; ask some questions first. Perhaps there was information you didn't know when you told them what you wanted done, and they had to adjust to new details you didn't know. Or maybe they had a brilliant idea for how to handle the situation you didn't think of.

Perhaps you thought your spouse was going to get a babysitter so you could enjoy a much-needed night out, only to come home and find that all is not as you expected. Before you get angry or think that your spouse does not value your time together, ask questions to find out what happened. Your spouse may not be feeling well, or the babysitter or one of the kids may be sick—you must get the facts before you jump to conclusions and explode.

These are just some examples, and I could go on and on, but you get the idea. Before you get angry, stop and get the facts. Make sure you understand all the facts. A side effect of doing this is that when you take the time to ask questions and get all the facts, you've also given yourself time to resist your first angry impulse and instead give a more reasonable, thought-out response.

What the Bible calls "outbursts of rage" are not really okay ever—we're never to be driven by our anger so much that we're out of control. It is not a sin to be angry (your children may have earned your anger and need to be corrected), but it is a sin to let your anger control you, and exploding is nearly always letting your anger control you.

Do You Get Defensive?

Asking questions before you decide whether or not your anger (or any other emotional reaction) is justified is a terrific step for defusing outbursts of rage. However, I want to flip this around, because when we are asked questions and we respond with anger, it can show another hidden anger problem.

You may need anger management if you are extremely defensive when people ask you questions.

When other people ask you questions, before they respond do you get defensive? If you feel the need to explain, justify, and fight back against questions you *think* may be leading somewhere you don't like, you may be dealing with an anger issue.

Sometimes people don't even have to say anything—we just have to *think* they're implying something and we get angry! When you are defensive a lot, you feel like people are criticizing you...even when they're not! They may be trying to ask questions before they decide how to respond, but you think they are asking leading questions, and you try to beat them to the punch by getting angry. This is a learned anger response: the preemptive strike. You think before they attack you, you should attack first, so you use your anger as a first strike weapon.

When we do this, we are not responding in love, and I have found that seeking God's love is one of the best ways to combat this kind of anger. Paul writes, "*Love is patient and kind. Love is not jealous or boastful or proud or rude. It does not demand its own way. It is not irritable, and it keeps no record of being wronged. It does not rejoice about injustice but rejoices whenever the truth wins out. Love never gives up, never loses faith, is always hopeful, and endures through every circumstance*" (1 Corinthians 13:4-7 NLT).

Love believes the best about every person. When we are defensive, we are expecting the worst of people and their intentions. If, instead, we looked to what God says about love and then asked Him to help us respond like that, we would react with God's love instead of defensively.

Do not let "project anger" from something someone else did cause you to be on the defensive now just because it reminds you of that person or situation. If you've been hurt, recognize it, grieve it, and then ask God for healing. Don't just keep being defensive because you are wounded and don't trust others and are seeking to protect yourself from getting hurt again. You know the Healer, so knock and keep on knocking for your healing, and replace that defensiveness with love.

Anger is not just outside the walls of our churches; it is inside the Church as well. One angry woman in my church was furious because she felt another woman across the aisle was staring at her impolitely. When it eventually came out that the woman across the aisle was actually looking for someone else, the woman who thought she'd been disrespected, and who had been so angry over it, was now embarrassed at her outburst of anger.

When I first got onto the radio locally, a Christian radio station that carried some of the best teachers in the world had fifteen-minute segments from me and some other local churches. Our ministry was growing in attendance and passion for the Lord, so we were blessed with a very good time slot. As people heard the radio broadcast, they would come visit the church, so the radio ministry was helping the church blossom.

Well, at one point, the ministry with the fifteen-minute slot directly after ours began using his time to contest the segment I taught. Apparently we had differences of denomination and doctrine, and I'll never forget my shock at hearing him try to attack my message.

Specifically, he took issue with anything that he felt was "prosperity." I believe that Christians ought to be blessed and your needs met, and for at least a week, this one-sided debate went on. He would take the fifteen-minute snippet of an hour-long message out of context and hotly try to counter it.

At first, I was mad. This was my first time being attacked like this, and I was indignant. However, God had already been working on my anger issues by this point. And so, when an opportunity presented itself to use the tools I'll be teaching you as the book progresses, I took it. I heard this other preacher asking for money on his program—which I thought was ironic, since he was spending his time trying to refute the prosperity gospel he thought I was teaching—and I felt like God moved on my heart to give to his ministry.

The Lord helped me let go of my offense and give to this man who was attacking our ministry. God helped me forgive, and then gave me the chance to put my money where my mouth was—to follow up my heart change with an action.

It is my experience that deep down we all want peace. However, many of us do not know how to make peace. It is a little like me wanting to make banana pudding: I can get out the little box, and I can read the recipe on the back, but when I make it, it does not taste the same as when my wife makes it. She knows things that I don't—basically, how to make it taste good.

There is more to wanting peace than simply trying to follow a list of ingredients. There are things about peace that many people don't know, or they don't know how to put it together. You can't make what you don't know, so even when you have all the right ingredients, you may not know how to put them together in a way that makes something good.

A good recipe is not just about ingredients but about the way you put things together. You can have too much salt or sugar in the cake.

Peace, in my humble opinion, is comprised of patience, understanding, love, and prayer.

It is hard to have peace when you are not patient. Hard to have peace when you don't have understanding (which is not agreement but is simply comprehension about my current situation). Love is the main ingredient in the life of a believer—love for people, as well as for ourselves and for God. God's people are a great recipe for peace.

You're Not Just an Angry Person

Some people justify their anger by saying, "This is just how I am."

That is a *lie*.

None of us were *born* angry, even redheads! None of us came out of our mothers' wombs angry; it is a learned behavior. You *became* angry, but *it is never who you are*. Stop ascribing this to your character.

You are a blood-bought child of God if you are in Christ, and you have the Holy Spirit. You can change your angry disposition if you *choose* to. I guarantee God wants to help you with this. He does not want children who are hurting themselves and others through their anger, and He will work with you to heal this place in your life and deal with this learned behavior.

You can get better, friend. And when you get better in this area, you will help others get better—in your house, at your job, and other angry people to whom you can minister after God has brought you through your own journey of healing. Others will be drawn to you instead of scared off by you, and there are practical things you can do today to start—things like asking questions before you respond and assuming the best of others until proven wrong.

God wants to help you here, and He has provided the wisdom of His Word, the blood of Jesus that redeemed you from the rule of sin and your flesh, and His Holy Spirit within you. His has promised His peace and power and blessing to you, and a life free of anger issues is so much sweeter than the bitter existence of being ruled by your negative emotions.

This book is designed to help you understand how these negative emotions affect you and others. Later in the book, I will give you a formula to overcome it, but first I want to look at *why* we're angry.

4

WHY ARE YOU ANGRY?

Hopefully in the last few chapters, you've seen a glimpse of yourself and your type of anger. I could have spent the whole rest of this book trying to profile anger and the ways we know we may need anger management, but I believe God gave me more to say than that.

I think it is worthwhile to take a moment to look at why we're angry. There are as many different individual reasons as there are people, but there are common themes you may already be seeing as I've given you examples over the last two chapters.

By every account, we appear to be an angry people. Quick to take offense, we find reasons for anger everywhere. Turn on the television, and you see constant reasons to get mad. From politics to racial tensions to the economy, injustice seems to be everywhere, and we hear about it more quickly and in more detail than ever before. As I've mentioned before, anger is not a male or female issue, and it is not limited to adults.

Much of our anger may be part of the times in which we live. We see new reasons to be angry everywhere; we have more information than ever before. Injustice, oppression, and exploitation still exist, and we have more ways of inciting and spreading our anger than ever before.

Social media can fan our anger in a way no society has ever experienced. We see what someone said, and we flare up. We're free to vent our opinions without consequence. Social media allows people to be angry without being responsible, because it offers a certain sense of anonymity. We will say things on social media about people that we would never say to their faces, and while we've become increasingly averse to confrontation, we are far more open to passive-aggressive social media commentary than ever before.

When you see that someone seems to have a nicer house, car, vacation, spouse, or family than you do, you may feel jealousy flare up. Anger is often right behind it. "Why don't *I* have that?" you might angrily pray. If you are thin-skinned and dealing with anger or jealousy issues, social media is something to be very careful with. It will fan up flames in you that may need to be under tighter control until you put them out completely. And the more successful you are, the higher profile you are, the more subject you are to active attacks on social media.

The ease with which we find new reasons to get angry or offended may touch on other sensitive areas in our lives. We seem to be angry as a culture, but within certain groups, anger is boiling just beneath the surface. Racial tension seems to have escalated anger over recent decades, and perhaps it was brought more into the spotlight with the election of our country's first African-American President, Barack Obama. Race or the specter of race was right at the surface of many political conversations for his entire tenure.

Perhaps not since the 1960s have we seen race so much at the forefront of discussion; and with it, anger—anger at mistreatment, at misunderstandings, at unequal rights or media coverage. Entire groups of people have been dealing with anger more obviously than at any time since the Civil Rights era.

Anger is birthed when there is a dichotomy—unequal treatment. And we more clearly see these contrasts now in our information-overload age than ever before.

Racially-charged shootings have polarized communities, even entire states, and anger at the injustices or even the perception of a double-standard has inflamed communities and given rise to all kinds of angry outbursts. Whether the events that set them off were wrong or not, these outbursts of rage are evidence of the anger that has been smoldering just beneath the calm surface, and it is our job, all of us, to see that the underlying issues are addressed and not just the things that set them off.

Right or wrong, justified or not, we are an angry people.

The Quest for Control

Perhaps one of the biggest underlying themes behind our anger is our desire for *control*. We often get angry when we are unable to control our circumstances or other people. We get frustrated when the person ahead of us makes poor driving decisions. We get angry when our children defy us. We get irritated when our plans get ruined.

Loss or lack of control can inspire a lot of anger.

In addition, sometimes we go off and explode because we feel that we *gain* a certain measure of control by acting out in our anger. I was in the store recently and watched one person get a favorable response from the customer service clerk when trying to return an item. Everyone stayed calm. However, the next woman didn't get what she wanted. I didn't hear the details, but she went *off*. She got loud and angry, and eventually in came the manager. In order to settle the problem and get this woman back under control, he did what she wanted.

When she didn't get the desired result and was not able to control the clerk's response, she got angry, and in getting angry, she got the result she wanted. Has this ever been your experience?

Control—the lack of it or the desire to get it—is one of the biggest triggers of anger I have found. Many angry people are simply hungry to control something—*anything*. I see angry children and teenagers who act out in the ways they feel are available to them, because there is something they can control. Girls who cut themselves, develop eating disorders, or dress provocatively; boys who disrupt their class, pursue sexual conquests, and take out their aggression on the football field—they're all symptoms of kids who feel a lack control over their lives, are angry, and are trying to exert control in the areas they feel they can.

Adults are no different. We seek things we can control, and we try to use them to make ourselves feel better. Anger can often be out of a desire for control.

Walking Wounded

Hurt is another big trigger of anger. The girl who cuts herself is hurting in an area of her life that she can't control, so she cuts herself because that's a pain she *can* control. She can't control the pain of her friends talking bad about her or what people think or how her father treats her, so she hurts herself to distract from the deeper pain. Instead of letting those things hurt her, she tries to regain control by hurting herself, and though the anger may not be on the surface, I assure you this poor girl is angry deep inside—angry at society, angry at her friends, angry at her family, angry at herself.

Anger is a common response when someone is hurting. There's a phrase: Wounded animals don't act right, and neither do hurting people.

How often do you get hurt and it flares into anger? When you bite the inside of your cheek or stub your toe and someone asks what's wrong, have you ever responded with angry words like, "Leave me alone!"? When hurt emotionally, have you ever lashed out, seething against whomever or whatever hurt you? It is a very common response.

Hurting people hurt other people. We see it in school shootings like Columbine, Virginia Tech, or Sandy Hook, but we also see it in parents who vent their frustrations on their kids, bosses who are jerks to their employees, and, yes, even pastors who stir up hatred or bigotry in their congregations. These are all hurting people who are then taking out their pain on others for ostracizing them, bullying them, ignoring them, or not giving them what they want.

Anger is behind the pain, because instead of sadness, we can often transpose our emotion into something that offers us more potential for regaining control. Being sad over a pain or a tragedy does not offer us the same illusion of regaining control, but anger seems to offer us the chance to *do something* with or about our pain.

Being sad makes us feel like victims; anger can make us feel like we're getting even.

There is no denying that life can sometimes be painful, and people, circumstances, and things can hurt us and disappoint us. We can get frustrated as we feel we're losing control. We can even feel hurt and frustrated with God when He doesn't do what we want, when we want, or when we feel He was responsible for causing or not preventing something bad from happening. And instead of feeling our pain and sadness and processing it, we get angry.

The problem with getting angry because we lack control or when we try to regain control by blowing up is that when we do these things, we're actually giving control *away*. We are giving our anger control.

One of the core scriptures for this book is Ephesians 4:26-27, which says, "'*Don't sin by letting anger control you.' Don't let the sun go down while you are still angry, for anger gives a foothold to the devil*" (NLT).

Letting anger control you is a sin. It gives a foothold to the devil, and while you think you are regaining control through anger, in fact you are giving your enemy control in your life.

We all get hurt. We all lose our feeling of control, and it is only natural to get frustrated and even angry. Yet when our anger becomes a means of trying to get control back, we have a problem.

One of the hallmarks of witchcraft is the manipulation of a person's will. God gives us free will and allows us to choose but does not manipulate our will to make us choose His ways. Though we do not think of it in these terms, we can try to control people with our anger. People may avoid doing things, saying things, or addressing things because they don't want you to be angry with them. You can use anger to get people to change their minds or redefine their will. Like blowing up over a trip to the mall or to a particular restaurant to get what you want, we can use our anger to control others. This kind of anger has a stigma like this attached, and people will say, "Let's not make them mad; you know how they are...."

Your Pain Has an Expiration Date

There is a proper way to deal with our loss of control and our pain, and if you've already given place to the devil and given him a measure of control in your life, you can learn how to handle these things God's way and to regain what the enemy has taken.

Sometimes we think it is through success, fame, fortune, or overcoming adversity—and all these things can be good things—but they will never substitute for truly dealing with your pain and your frustration at your loss of control. Those are all Band-Aids if they're trying to treat the underlying problem; eventually they're going to tear off and expose that your wound has become infected and toxic.

I have performed many funerals, and I have counseled with many people who've lost someone dear to them. There are many stages to grief, and everyone experiences it differently, but I tell them all that it is vital they give themselves time and permission to grieve properly. Grief is a process, and so is hurt—we must give ourselves permission to experience our pain, grieve it, and let it sadden us before we think about moving on.

If you hold onto your hurt too long, it becomes unhealthy, but it is also unhealthy to shunt your pain and disappointment into anger instead of letting it sadden you and properly mourning it. But you can't sit in your hurt forever—all kinds of bad things will come from that, like depression and inappropriate ways of acting out like anger and revenge.

Grief, like food, is good *for a time*. It is good to allow ourselves permission to experience it and to give ourselves time to heal. But if we just cover it over and store it away, pain can spoil and turn toxic.

Like leftovers, your hurt has an expiration date, my friend, and before you reach that point, it is time to get rid of it. God has good promises for you on the other side of your hurt and pain, when you've dealt with your anger.

You can contain your grief and your hurt, and you can keep it, but at some point you have to throw it out. In fact, if you keep it too long, it can become truly dangerous. That's what has happened to these people who have acted out violently; they tried to contain their hurt, and it became toxic to the point of being dangerous—even deadly.

When we move past our hurt, we make room for the new thing God desires to do in our lives. Isaiah 43:19 says, *"Behold, I will do a new thing, now it shall spring forth; shall you not know it? I will even make a road in the wilderness and rivers in the desert."* If your life has been consumed with hurt or anger, you are on your way to becoming a desert wilderness, devoid of green, life-giving things and full of only dryness and even death.

Maybe you've lost someone dear to you, like a spouse or a father figure. There is no denying you're hurt. Give yourself time to grieve properly, but be open to God showing you the expiration date on your mourning. God has good plans for you—plans to give you a hope and a future. But if you are closed off, contained in your grief and giving place to your anger, you are giving a foothold to the devil for him to gain control over your life. If, instead, you give that hurt to God and let Him begin a healing work, you can let Him bring hope for a brighter, healthier future.

A wonderful Psalm says, *"Weeping may endure for a night, but joy comes in the morning"* (Psalm 30:5b). You may be in a period of darkness, sadness, and anger, but joy comes in the morning.

Let Go of the Pain of the Past

You may agree with me that letting go of your hurt or frustration at your loss of control sounds wonderful, but you may not know *how* to do that. The latter portion of this book is going to focus on how to move past these things, but I want to give you some of it now.

Your hurt has a time frame, and I want to encourage you to pray and seek God for the expiration date—whether you've exceeded it or not. Ask Him if you have shunted your pain and hurt into anger, rather than grieving it properly. If you haven't yet really allowed yourself to feel sad, do so. Experience this healthy emotion, and don't try to move it to something else and avoid it. Dealing with our pain is not easy, but it is an important part of recovering from what has hurt us.

After you grieve your hurt, then it is time to start picking up the pieces. Often, we need help doing this when we've been badly hurt. Don't be afraid or embarrassed to ask for help from trustworthy and godly people—your pastor, a Christian counselor, and trusted and spiritual mature friends can all be brothers and sisters who can help safely and appropriately.

Next, you may need to get it straight with God. If you've been stewing in your toxic hurt long after the expiration date, you probably have some forgiveness to ask for, both from God and from others. We read in 1 John 1:9, "*If we confess our sins, He is faithful and just to forgive us our sins and to cleanse us from all unrighteousness.*"

Own up to your actions, confess your sin to God, and determine to turn away from that course. Turning away from a bad course is called *repentance*, and it is more than feeling sorry for having done the wrong thing—it is turning around and going the other direction.

This will probably involve apologizing for the wrong things you've done in your pain and anger. When it is safe to do so, ask the people you've hurt for their forgiveness—even if you don't think they will give it to you. You may also need to *forgive yourself*. We sometimes ignore this important step and think that we somehow need to hold ourselves in a penalty box until we've demonstrated to God and others that we're good and truly sorry. Release yourself.

Finally, it is time to try to take steps to help prevent it from happening again, if possible. We cannot control all circumstances and events around us, but we can control ourselves. If you have an anger problem, it is important to deal with the root. Circumstances may set you off, but I guarantee that under the surface is something deeper than the current problem you exploded about. I will be teaching you more tools for dealing with the root as this book goes on, but this is work that is at first going on largely between you and God. He will work on you as you spend time with Him in prayer, reading the Scriptures, praying in the Spirit, and even by speaking to the godly people in your life.

God will show you where you went wrong, such as by ignoring the expiration date, and together you can put in place practical things to help you next time such as learning a lifestyle of forgiveness and thankfulness, accountability and submission, and being in Christian community.

No matter why you are angry, God has a path forward for you that leads to a good future full of blessings and promises. He wants to do a new thing in you, my friend, and it will bring life to the toxic desert of anger the enemy has tried to create in you. Instead, God will make a path forward for you and streams of refreshment to sustain you along the way.

5
WHAT TYPE OF ANGRY ARE YOU? PASSIVE OR JUDGMENTAL

Understanding that we have an anger problem is such an important first step, and I hope that the early chapters of this book helped you open up to the idea you and God may have some work to do. We are in an angry society, and too often we look to our anger to give us power and control or keep us from losing those things.

When you've come to terms with the fact that giving place to our anger surrenders control by giving it to your enemy, it can be very helpful to identify what types of anger you deal with. It will help you notice when you are relinquishing power in your life to the enemy of your soul.

Let me say that these are not exactly what you will find in a psychology textbook. It is not my intention to replace those kinds of studies. Remember, we are not interested in traditional "anger management." We are learning to deal with our anger God's way, and we're learning to identify it when we see it in ourselves. With that understanding in place, let's look at the first type of anger I want to cover.

Passive Anger

Passive anger is not the brash, overt emotion that we often think of when we talk about anger. If your definition of anger looks like bulging eyes, a red face, and screaming, you may misidentify passive anger, but it is very common and no less damaging if we give place to it.

I bring it up first, however, because it may be the most "holy" kind and the hardest to identify. In fact, many people with this type of anger problem would likely argue that they do not, in fact, have an anger problem at all. They would say that their behavior is just part of their personality or even their sense of humor. Because they aren't loud and obvious, they may feel they're managing or control their anger better than someone who simply explodes.

Instead of going off, people with passive anger let it out slowly, covertly (so they think), and in more subtle ways. You have perhaps heard of passive-aggressive anger, which is where the normally passive person suddenly vents. While this is definitely possible, many people dealing with this variety of anger may not ever explode. They may just leak, often through comments, their anger out over time.

Do you like sarcasm? Do you love a great retort, a witty come-back, or a clever response? Do you like verbal jabs? Would people, or yourself, call you sharp tongued? If so, this may be your variety of anger. Passive anger doesn't explode at you—they slip little barbs and jabs in, and they use sarcasm frequently, trying to veil their angry responses under the guise of humor.

Passive anger people will cut you up with their words—but some-times only inside their minds! They're not physically intimidating, but they may be snide, taking digs and shots at people, again, often under pretense of, "I was just joking."

It might help to think of the stereotypical Jewish mother on TV—always with a comment that cuts someone down without officially being so offensive that it starts a fight. They have a great sense for how far they can push it, and they will let their angry comments vent only in limited amounts so they don't outright provoke anyone. And if they do, they will passively back off, claiming their comments weren't intentional or that they weren't trying to be mean or angry.

We see this many times in groups of friends where commentary is made in jest but it is a way to tell you how they feel. Currently this is called "shade." It is a nonconfrontational way to express one's feeling of hurt, disappointment, or disagreement without being confrontational.

While someone with aggressive anger may try to bludgeon what they want out of people with loud outbursts of rage, people with passive anger rely on their sharp wit and tongue to get what they want. A quick barb, a subtle taunt, a veiled insult, a witty come-back—these are the tools people with passive anger use.

We'll explore general answers to the anger issue later in the book, but let's look at some practical tips for those who struggle with passive anger. First, you need to learn to recognize that what they are doing is, in truth, anger. It can be a slow-burning, more subtle form of anger and much harder to identify, so it is very important to ask the Holy Spirit to search your heart and expose whether or not you have trouble with this type of anger. Do not let yourself off with a casual thought that you don't have a problem because you are not loud; allow the Holy Spirit to search your heart and show you what the results are. Only then can you start down a path toward freedom.

Passively angry people can make a great deal of progress in dealing with their anger by watching their tongues. James talks extensively about the power of the tongue. Like a bridle or the rudder of a ship, the tongue is small, but it can control or change the course of our lives. This small thing, he tells us, can be the tiny spark that sets off a forest fire (see James 3:5-6). And if you think that your tiny passive, sarcastic barbs don't do real damage, you completely underestimate the power of your tongue and are in for a rude surprise one day!

As surely as a spring should not bubble with fresh water and bitter water, a life honoring Jesus should not produce both blessings and these flames of fire from our tongues. They have the power to defile us, and we should not use them to both bless and curse—through the power of the Holy Spirit, we must put our spirits in charge of our tongues!

If this is you—if you are a person with passive anger—repent today. Decide to turn away from this type of anger, and give God control of your tongue. Ask for the Holy Spirit is help to put your spirit, not your angry emotions, in charge of your tongue, and begin using it only to bless and not to cut down. Surrender that part of yourself to God, and forsake your sharp tongue in favor of a tongue that deals out blessings only.

The prayer for the person of passive anger is, "*Create in me a clean heart, O God...*" (Psalm 51:10).

Judgmental Anger

The next type of anger I want to discuss is judgmental anger. Again, these aren't the people who go off and explode; these are the hurting, jealous, or resentful people who are so bitter or wounded that when they see good things happening to others, judgmental and hurting comments knife out of their lips.

Do you get angry or jealous when you see someone with a new car—especially someone you think doesn't deserve it or won't enjoy it properly? Perhaps a little old woman in a sports car makes you wonder, "Why does she have that kind of car? She's not going to get the enjoyment out of it." (Unstated is the addition, "...like I would.") When you see someone's Facebook post about a vacation, do you immediately compare their vacation to yours? Or your *lack* of a vacation? Do you feel a stab of resentment that their children have nicer clothes or are going to more activities or doing better in school than yours are? Do they have a nicer yard than yours? Bigger house? Better toys? Do you compare, and then find your life comes up wanting? Do you find yourself often disappointed or regretful? If these seem to apply, you may be dealing with judgmental anger.

Judgmental anger is the anger of the suburbs—it is jealousy speaking, and this form of anger is very common today. It is the anger of comparison.

I want to spend a moment more here. I mentioned social media earlier in the book, and if you find that you have this form of anger, you need to avoid social media until God has dealt with this in your life. Social media provides a breeding ground for this kind of anger and gives it the ideal environment to grow and expand.

Consider this: We put only our best things on social media—our biggest triumphs, proudest moments, and grandest successes. Rarely if ever do you see anyone post anything less than their best. But for every photo or post, you know—because you've likely done it—that the photo that looks so perfect and casual is actually staged, and it took ten to get it right! It is said that comparing our lives to others on social media is like holding our behind-the-scenes footage up against their highlight reel. It is never going to match up, because you know all your dirty little secrets, failings, and shortcomings. Consciously, you know others have these problems too, but subconsciously, we see and compare these social media highlights and judge others and ourselves harshly, often without even knowing it.

Like passive anger, judgmental anger can be hard to identify. You may not even vent it—or if you do, it may sound more like complaining or wishful thinking than outright anger and jealousy. We learn to sanitize it, even Christianize it, so that our comments don't drip with judgmentalism and covetousness.

When you judge something, you are making a pronouncement about it. When you can't be happy for someone else's success or applaud them doing well—and instead of rejoicing with them you are saying or thinking jealous, resentful things—you are pronouncing a judgment on them.

Think back to what we read in James about our tongues. If you are not using your tongue to rejoice with others, are you using it to pronounce judgment against them? If so, be careful; that is very much like a curse. Matthew 7:1-2 tells us, *"Judge not, that you be not judged. For with what judgment you judge, you will be judged; and with the measure you use, it will be measured back to you."*

Comparison is at the heart of this anger, and the root of comparison is pride, which we will explore in more depth later. It is pride to think that God should treat you differently than He does because of how He is treating someone else. Paul writes to the believers in Corinth, *"For we dare not class ourselves or compare ourselves with those who commend themselves. But they, measuring themselves by themselves, and comparing themselves among themselves, are not wise"* (2 Corinthians 10:12).

Take the time to turn in your Bible to Romans 12 and read it for yourself if this is your type of anger. I draw your attention to verse 3: *"Don't think you are better than you really are. Be honest in your evaluation of yourselves, measuring yourselves by the faith God has given us."* Romans 12:14-15: *"Bless those who persecute you; bless and do not curse. Rejoice with those who rejoice, and weep with those who weep."*

The Key of Thankfulness

One other scriptural reference comes to mind as we talk about judgmental anger is a cautionary tale. We are familiar with the story of the prodigal son, and countless messages have been taught about avoiding his folly. However, his elder brother was foolish in another way. When he hears his brother has come home, the elder brother will not go in to the lavish welcome party the father throws. When the father asks him about it, he replies, *"All these years I've slaved for you and never once refused to do a single thing you told me to. And in all that time you never gave me even one young goat for a feast with my friends. Yet when this son of yours comes back after squandering your money on prostitutes, you celebrate by killing the fattened calf!"* (Luke 15:29-30 NLT).

What do you hear in his words? Comparison. Resentment. Jealousy. Judgment.

Now, read the father's reply: *"Son, you are always with me, and all that I have is yours"* (Luke 15:31).

This is the Father's reply to you, dear reader. If you are in Christ, everything He has belongs to you, and from you He withholds no good thing. Release this anger; repent of it. End its control over you, because by holding people in judgment and jealousy, you are not hurting them or God's blessing over them one bit—the only one you are hurting is yourself.

It is hard to realize this form of anger is influencing or controlling you. No one likes to find out they're being jealous and resentful, but it is vital that you are honest with yourself and let God search your heart.

That is the first step, but another important component to overcoming this anger is thankfulness. An entire section of this book deals with the tool of thankfulness, but let me touch briefly on it here, because if this is the type of anger that is controlling you, thankfulness is the key to your prison.

Choose to be happy with what God has given you right now—your lot, whatever it is. That does not mean you cannot desire to do better; but while you are dealing with this anger, you must set that aside and choose thankfulness instead.

When I first started preaching, I was envious of the pastors who had more members in their churches. The truth of the matter was, *I was not ready* to have that many people coming to my church. If God gave you exactly what you are dreaming about today, you may not be ready for it, and you'd spoil His good gift.

Choose to embrace a season of celebrating others' success. Reject comparison. If that means restricting or shutting down social media for a season—or for good!—do it while God works on this issue with you. Learn to be happy with what you have.

I did a sermon series a while back called *How to Have a Happy Life* that would probably bless you and is available on our website. The first step I gave was learning to be happy with what you have. Learn to celebrate others. Stop comparing yourself to others. Count your blessings. Learn to give. These are just a few of the things that will help this type of anger lose its hold over you and restore your happiness.

For me personally, that looked like deciding to be what I call "house poor." That meant that while we could have afforded a bigger house, we decided to choose a smaller house so we could take care of other priorities. That was all well and good...until we later saw people buying bigger, fancier houses or we'd go to dinner and see where someone else lived. We had to remind ourselves that we were choosing to be happy with where we were.

But when that season was over, we were able to enjoy the next without having bad experiences that hung over our head. We embraced celebrating what God was doing in others' lives, choosing to rejoice with them when God blessed them. We knew that God is the giver of all good gifts, and in time He would bless us, too.

The prayer for the person with judgmental anger is this: "Father, I recognize my error in being judgmental, and I ask You to forgive me. Holy Spirit, help me in this area. The Word of God says You are my helper and I allow You space in my life to help me with this. I now choose to respond with joy and kindness at the success of others, knowing that my turn will come one day. Thank You, Lord, in Jesus' name. Amen."

Be Transformed

Let me emphasize here that I am not simply advocating a better attitude as the solution to your anger problem. Along with watching your words if you deal with passive anger, simply changing what you say by sheer willpower or deciding to be thankful, in and of themselves, are not going to remake your heart. True change requires the work of the Holy Spirit.

The keys to dealing with your anger are recognizing that you deal with it and then repenting of it and turning away. The practical steps I'm describing are the "turning away" part, but without the help of the Holy Spirit, behavior change will be temporary or only skin deep. True change in these areas of our lives begins and ends with the redemptive, life-changing work of the Holy Spirit remaking us from the inside out.

Earlier I showed you some scriptures from Romans 12, but now I want to present to you the one that makes those others possible—the one that makes any part of our Christian walk possible: "*Do not be conformed to this world, but be transformed by the renewing of your mind, that you may prove what is that good and acceptable and perfect will of God*" (Romans 12:2).

Replacing your type of anger with God's blessing on your life is not a matter of more effort, discipline, or willpower. It is the natural effect of being transformed into a new person by letting God change the way you think, react, and behave. The behavior follows the heart change, so determine today to forsake your old ways of handling your anger, which are delivering you into bondage to the enemy and giving him a foothold. Instead, allow God to transform your life into something that is good, pleasing, and perfect to Him.

6
WHAT TYPE OF ANGRY ARE YOU? OVERWHELMED OR AGGRESSIVE

Overwhelmed anger is caused by life demanding more than someone can cope with. It comes from a state of being swamped under—not just for a single interaction, an hour, or a day of trouble, but from days, weeks, months, or even *years* of feeling overwhelmed by life. Depression is very common for this type of situation, but eventually for many it turns to quick bursts of anger. These are not the calculated jabs like the passive person or a general low-grade cynicism like the judgmental person; they're knee-jerk responses that come from continually being pushed past your limits.

Overwhelmed anger often manifests like quick losses of control—sudden outbursts from a person who is too stressed, too busy, or too drained to respond more reasonably. They're like a little dog that growls or snaps when startled; they snap when pushed just a little bit because they have no margin. They're living in a state of over-whelmed, and any extra thing is simply too much for them.

My friend, the devil cannot stop you, but he can make you *busy*. If a whole legion of demons could not keep the demoniac at the tombs of Geneseret from coming to Jesus, the enemy cannot stop you, a blood-bought child of God. But if he cannot stop you, he can distract you. He can con you into taking on too much. When you are too busy, you open yourself to this type of anger.

Overwhelmed anger is a major problem for our over-busy, frantic, multitasking society. We are stretched too thin, moving too fast, and trying to do too much—and it frays us at the edges until we just snap. Overwhelmed anger is often caused by simply trying to do too much.

However, there are times people are beset by circumstances outside their control that stretched them past their limits. When we lose a loved one, a career, or our life savings, as well as a host of other things, it can create an environment of overwhelmed. This can also be a source of anger. You'll remember what I said earlier about hurts and wounds—people hurting like this can lash out, because they are hurt and simply overcome by the difficulties they're facing. But all too often, we exist in a state of overwhelmed anger not because of great tragedies but because we're overcommitted and have no margin.

I've met so many moms who feel they have to be Wonder Woman—everywhere all the time, everything for everyone, and always going, going, going. They hold themselves to impossible standards, and when they, their families, their houses, or their jobs don't measure up, they feel like failures. They're so stressed and pressed, sometimes it just takes one little thing to finally crack their incredible patience. Maybe she works a job where she deals with workplace stress all day only to come home, handle the kids, and start fixing dinner. Or maybe she spends the day cleaning the house, running the kids to their numerous events, changing the baby, and cooking. But her single girlfriend calls with a boyfriend crisis, Jimmy gets in trouble at school, and the baby has a blowout with no change of clothes while they're at the grocery store. Normally loving, inexhaustible mom simply gets pushed too far, and when she goes off, you don't want to be around to deal with the fallout! She ends up offending her friend, being short with Jimmy's teacher, and screaming in the parking lot of the grocery store loud enough that an employee pushing carts back in looks ready to run.

Men try to be Superman. They work long hours, throwing themselves into their jobs and trying to make a living and climb the ladder. They want to give good things to their families, so they grind themselves to the bone at work. All day, they deal with crisis after crisis, demands on them from every corner, and all the while they keep their business face on. They feel the pressure to not just get by but to be successful, to get the promotion, and to get ahead or to get the nice car, the boat, the lake house, or just take a vacation. Then, they come home…and it is simply too much. All he wants to do is close his eyes for two minutes and breathe, but Jimmy needs help with his homework and Suzie needs to go to dance recital. Both are talking, or arguing, and his wife wants him to take out the trash. Suddenly, he just explodes! This man loves his family, but after the long day it is just too much for him, and he snaps, injuring his relationship with his children and wife.

Or maybe it is a difficult season. You've experienced a loss in the family, and you wonder how long your five-year-old will even remember Grandma. Maybe you lose your health in a battle with heart disease or cancer, and every day for months and even years is just a struggle to survive. Perhaps your job, which never seemed to be quite enough to cover your expenses before, falls through and you get laid off, and now you have no idea how you are going to make ends meet because you are already overextended financially.

Then, something *else* happens…and it is just too much! You snap at someone for asking how you are doing after your loss, you are rude to the nurse who just doesn't understand, or scream at the ATM because you are overdrawn. For you, maybe all those things happen in one day!

Does any of this sound like you? You're just pressed to the breaking point…and then something else hits. You're overwhelmed. And when someone pricks you, you aren't full of compassion and patience; you are full of frustration and anger.

The Perfect Word: "No"

A lot of this form of anger comes from unrealistic expectations upon ourselves. As I mentioned, we try to be super—to be *perfect*. We want things to go perfectly in our lives, and we'll work and struggle to get them there until we're so strained and worn out we break down. We think we must be at every meeting, every game, every social function; we think we need everything we see around us and to give our kids every advantage that we didn't have. We want the house to be clean all the time, the yard to always be lush and mowed, our kids to be constantly well-groomed and polite, and we never want to disappoint anyone—including God and ourselves.

Many of us are simply overcommitted. We've bitten off more than we can chew because we think that's what we're supposed to do to be a good parent or child, employee or boss, church member or pastor. We put all this weight on our shoulders...and it is crushing us.

I want to give you a couple of very practical tips, but also some spiritual ones. The first is that I want to teach you a *magic word* for dealing with overwhelmed anger.

It is the word "*No.*"

This is truly a magical, powerful word. It is freeing, empowering, and life-giving. We're taught it is a bad word, an impolite word, and will make us evil or hated, but it is actually a key to freeing yourself from the expectations of the world around you and yourself that are crushing you and driving you straight to overwhelmed anger.

You don't have to make every meeting—the company will survive one without you. You don't have to be at every game—your children are not going to need therapy because you messed up your perfect record. You don't have to go to every social event—your friends can make it without you. And, as shocking as this is to hear from a pastor, you don't have to be at church every time the doors are open. When these things are a blessing to you, you are free to do them; when they're the source of your overcommitted, stressed-out, and anger-generating lifestyle, sometimes you simply should say, "No," and take some time to recharge.

You've taken on more than God intended for you to have, and it is crushing the life out of you. If you are trying to do everything, you are probably doing nothing well. It is time to stop the chaos, focus on your priorities, and get your house in order.

Put God at the Center

Biblical priorities look like God first, then family, then work, and then friends. To some this means putting time with God first in the day, and it can mean that; but it also means putting Him first in *everything* you do. God is at the center—everything starts with Him, and as Robert Morris says, when you give Him the first and best, the rest is blessed.

Take the time to read all of Matthew 6, a loaded chapter of some of Jesus' most life-giving teaching. After teaching us how to pray, He addresses some of the things that can cause us the most stress: the trappings of this life. Jesus then explains why we should not worry, and then He brings it all home with this verse: "*But seek first the kingdom of God and His righteousness, and all these things shall be added to you*" (Matthew 6:33).

I'm not telling you to pray for four hours every day; I'm telling you to get your priorities straightened out. Start with God—put Him first. Then, get your home straight. You want the place you lay your head to be one of peace, so bring your "seek God first" mentality to your house—to your family. Then, take your focus on God with you to work, and finally, take Him with you to your friendships. Whatever you do, carry God with you as your first and singular priority.

Make time to be still and know that He is God. When we're constantly moving, we have no time for this, so say no to a few things until you have created a space to welcome God in your days. In that time together with Him, take Paul's advice: *"Don't worry about anything; instead, pray about everything. Tell God what you need, and thank him for all he has done. Then you will experience God's peace, which exceeds anything we can understand. His peace will guard your hearts and minds as you live in Christ Jesus"* (Philippians 4:6-7 NLT).

The prayer for the person with overwhelmed anger is that the peace of God, which surpasses your ability to understand it, will guard your heart and mind as you *live in Christ Jesus*. Don't just visit Him in the morning; *live* with Him. Welcome Him into every moment of every day, and put that first before anything else. You'll find that your overwhelmed anger begins to cool, because God's peace replaces the chaos that has been tormenting you.

Aggressive Anger

I have saved aggressive anger for now because it is probably the most dangerous. Aggressive anger can ruin your life very quickly because it has so much potential for destruction of lives and relationships.

Aggressive anger tends to occur in very hurt people. Often, someone modeled it for them, and they are emulating what they saw. Typically, those with aggressive anger have themselves been abused by it—they have experienced it firsthand, and they may hate it, but they find themselves doing it too. These are hurt people, deeply wounded by trauma, and they need healing. In their pain, they lash out, and without help they perpetuate a cycle of abusive anger into future generations.

People dealing with an aggressive form of anger are volatile, even dangerous. You may not think of yourself as such, but if your anger manifests in frequently losing control and breaking things, lashing out loudly and verbally, taking physical action, and saying hurtful, destructive things, your anger is aggressive and can become dangerous to yourself and others around you.

Aggressive anger is one of the two types for which I strongly recommend getting professional help while you deal with it—*now*, not later! People dealing with this need Christian counseling and to begin meeting with their pastors, because dealing with it by themselves hasn't worked, and it is time to act before someone gets hurt or does something that they permanently regret.

Remember, you can put the house back together again after you've destroyed it, and people may even forgive you, but they will not forget—they can't afford to. You can fill in the hole in the drywall you punched, but you cannot mend broken bones or bruises nearly as easily.

The distinctive thing about aggressive anger is this physical component. Do you physically lash out? Do you hit things when angry—even break things? Have you broken things that you regretted? Have you cost others or yourself money and respect because you broke something and had to replace it? Do you lose control? Do you do more than raise your voice, yelling and screaming in your anger? Do you make others cry? Have you ever touched another person in anger or threatened to? Has anyone ever fled the house or felt they needed to get away from your anger to stay safe? Have you ever had to be restrained, like having the police called or someone else who had to come in and intervene?

If so, you are dealing with aggressive anger, and you need to take steps right away to deal with it.

Aggressively angry people can lash out suddenly and with little or no warning, violently reacting to things others say or do quickly and even unpredictably. It can often be tied to substances, such as alcohol and drugs, but it may not be; it may be a learned behavior and a means of getting control. As with all these forms of anger, men and women can both deal with aggressive anger, but men are typically more dangerous because they can be bigger and stronger.

Physical manifestations are what set aggressive anger apart and make it so dangerous. Punching the wall or smashing something or screaming and cussing leads to a slippery slope that can degenerate quickly into physical and verbal abuse very suddenly. People with the early stages of aggressive anger often think that will never happen, and when it does, it was an accident and they're very sorry. But once it has happened, it will happen again, guaranteed.

Aggressive anger is an absolute deal breaker for relationships. Single people, if you suspect that the person you are dating may have aggressive anger, cut it off. It is that serious! They are not someone to be with—not until they deal with their stuff. Years from now, if they've dealt with it and you should happen to meet again, you can talk; but if they're dealing with it right now, *get out* of that relationship. It is not worth it—emotionally or physically.

If he's ever laid a hand on you in anger, he has crossed a line that must never, ever be crossed. It is completely unacceptable, and for your sake and for the sake of those you love and may need to protect, you must get to a place of safety. It will not get better, and you cannot fix him—period. Let go, move on, and pray for him from a distance.

For married people, if it has happened more than once, it is a deal breaker. Safety comes first for you and your family, and while your duty as a wife is to honor and respect and pray for your husband, you can do so from a place of safety. Whether or not he deals with his anger is between Him and God, but how *you* deal with his anger is between you, him, God, and your family, and you carry an extra burden to ensure they are *safe*.

If his aggressive anger has scared you, get safe, and get help. Contact a Christian counselor, tell people you can trust and who will help you, and speak with your pastor. The shame or embarrassment does not outweigh the danger of continuing in that environment, because once it has manifested physically, aggressive anger will go there again untreated and unchecked. You owe it to yourself to get impartial, wise, godly help and counsel.

I've read too many stories of the longsuffering wife who puts up with his angry outbursts again and again. When he's done, he's sorry, sure—he doesn't want to get caught! He doesn't want to pay the consequences for his action. So she lets him sweet-talk her, and she tries to forgive and forget. This is called "battered woman syndrome," and it can end up with someone *dead* or beaten—and it might not be you. It may be your daughter or your son. You need to put a stop to it by taking care of your family, regardless of your feelings toward him or the smooth lines he gives you.

If the person with aggressive anger in your life will not get help, you can think about leaving him for good, for the sake of yourself and your family, but we all have made mistakes. If that's genuinely what it was in the impartial mind of your godly counselors, and it was circumstantial and he's willing to repent and has gotten help, once you've established healthy boundaries and have a plan of action, you can work on your relationship. Until then, you must love and respect him in your heart—from a safe distance. If you've been touched by aggressive anger, forgiving and working the steps in this book can be helpful, but again, you do not need to expose yourself to further risk or injury to do so.

If you are the person manifesting aggressive anger, it is time to get help. Call someone like your pastor or a counselor immediately. *Take action* to protect your family *now*. It is time to repent of those actions and take a step the other way—that means taking steps to prevent this from happening, getting help and accountability, and manning up enough to put others ahead of your pride. Is it embarrassing? Yes. Is it humiliating? Yes.

Is it *lifesaving*? Definitely!!!

You owe it to your family, and yourself, to do whatever it takes to prevent this from happening again or escalating.

If it has happened once, under extreme stress or danger, it may be a fluke that you should be very wary about. But if you've taken physical action in your anger more than once, you need to contact a counselor, get on the phone with your pastor, and get into relationships that will hold you accountable to take, and continue taking, action to deal with this, and you need to do it right now.

Find what triggers you. Alcohol? Drugs? Unresolved wounds? The tools in this book are for you, too, but they are to add to and complete what you are going to do with a counselor; they're not a substitute.

If you are reading this and thinking that though you have this anger problem, it is under control and you can keep a lid on it, you are fooling yourself. You have nothing to lose from seeking help, and you have much to gain. Not only that, it may save a relationship—or even a life!

Judge Change by the Lasting Fruit

I have seen restoration take place. I have seen people change. I have seen a man who went away for decades for murder come out of prison a different man—because he let God work on him on the inside while he was "inside." No one can do it for you, but nothing is impossible for you and God.

We judge change by the fruit. The fruit of this man's life was love, joy, peace, patience, kindness, goodness, and self-control—a far cry from the angry, murdering young man he was. He demonstrated the evidence of his change through his fruit, and you must hold yourself or your man to the same standard. When you see the fruit of his change, you can start believing it; when you start demonstrating the fruit of your change, you can begin working on things like your relationship, because you know you are safe.

Show you have changed with your track record. That is how you judge if someone is safe to reassociate with—the fruit in their life.

As I mentioned at the beginning of this book, there were angry people in the Bible—and God still used them. Just because you've experienced this kind of anger, it doesn't mean you are disqualified, God is angry with you, or you can never repair the damage you've done. However, it does mean that you must start now by taking decisive action. Anger like this is a learned response, so if you learned it, you can unlearn it. You renounce it, turn away from it, and learn new, healthy behaviors to replace it. You can leave this anger behind, my friend.

Nothing is so manly as doing what needs to be done—taking the action necessary now, today, to stop this before someone gets hurt or hurt again.

My prayer for you is that your pride will not get in the way of getting help. I ask the Lord to help you see your need and that you will act while you are properly motivated. I pray that you find healing for whatever wound is at the heart of your pain and rage and that you allow God's love to minister to you. Lay your anger down, friend; you don't need it anymore. That season is over, and a new day has dawned.

In the next chapter I want to look at one final form of anger as well as looking at the consequences of *not* dealing with our anger. I know from experience that some reading this still are in denial—they think their anger isn't that serious, because they're not aggressively angry. But not owning up and dealing with this issue will cause significant problems down the line, and God has a better plan for you than that! He has power, love, peace, and grace He wants you to experience—the blessing of the Lord. If those sound good, read on with me, because great blessings await those who deal with this problem God's way.

7
THE PRICE OF ANGER

We have looked at four types of anger—passive, judgmental, overwhelmed, and aggressive. But now I want to examine one more, which has grave consequences to your life.

Chronic anger is anger that is constant. It is ever-present, like a dull throb, perhaps just under the surface of your life. People with chronic anger are perpetually angry and resentful, and they take a bitter, jaded approach to the world. The key to understanding it is the bitterness; it is anger that has gone from a circumstantial problem that spikes up to a deeply-rooted problem that has caused something in your heart to go toxic.

A root of bitterness causes chronic anger.

Chronically angry people have often experienced severe disappointment, hurt, shame, or other trauma that they have not properly dealt with. The expiration date came and went long, long ago, and now the hurt they've been holding onto has spoiled and rotted and embittered their heart. They never seem happy with others or themselves or life around them, and they let everyone know it. They're frequently defensive and quick to take offense.

This is a different level of anger than the others we've talked about so far. It is deeper, because it has taken root. These aren't seeds we're trying to keep from bearing fruit; the fruit is here, and it is *bad*.

People dealing with chronic anger have likely experienced other forms of anger for a long time but without properly dealing with it. They stuffed their passive, judgmental, or overwhelmed anger for so long, it has become second nature to them to experience these emotions. They've held onto the hurtful events, feelings, and responses a long time, and they long ago went bad and started poisoning their lives from deep inside.

Chronically angry people may be numb or just exist in a bad mood, grinding and grating through life with friction against absolutely every-thing. Every event, statement, and action goes through a souring filter, affecting every input they receive. None of it cheers them up, nothing seems positive, and nothing anyone can do helps them.

If you are chronically angry, you probably don't even want to be helped and resent it when people try. I hope you will read on, however, because there is help to be had.

I have great compassion for you if this is where you find yourself. If this is your type of anger, you've been hurt a long time without dealing with your wounds, and it has formed a bitter root within you. I am not saying you are a victim, but I am saying that someone has to be very, very hurt for a long time to become a chronically angry person. The good news is that there's hope for you!

If you are dealing with another type of anger, read about chronic anger as a cautionary tale. This is what will happen if you never take any action. It will ruin the good in your life, and you will often drive the people around you away because of it. Giving place to this bitter root will often leave you lonely and depressed as well as angry, and this type of anger is one of the two for which I really urge you to seek professional help.

If you've gotten to this dark place, you need to work closely with the Lord to dig up your bitter root, but you will likely be unable to do so alone. You will need strong Christian helpers who are willing to put up with your attitude while you dig out the root of the problem through intensive prayer and time with the Lord. Also, I suggest that professional counseling is in order for this type of anger. It is so set, so engrained, separating it from *you* and moving on from it will take time and expertise.

The key component to this is action—chronic anger is the result of never dealing with your anger and its root causes, so the solution is to finally take action. Drop your pride, surrender that unforgiveness and bitter root, and get help. There are many excellent Christian counselors, loving pastors, and other helpers who can bring experience and wisdom in the Lord to your circumstance and who will help you climb out of your pit, but often because it took time to get here, it takes time to get out.

The key to this is forgiveness, which we will explore more deeply in another chapter. For now, know that forgiveness starts with a *choice*. Long before you feel like forgiving, you can choose to forgive. You can choose to let go of the bitter root within you, surrender it to God, and ask Him to begin the work in your life.

Digging Up the Bitter Root

A bitter root is typically generated by an offense we have failed to forgive or let go. This seed of unforgiveness takes root in the soul and begins to affect the way we see similar situations. Once we have been this way for some time, it can be hard for us to let go of it, talk about it, or forgive because it has taken root. We may need to speak the words of forgiveness in this area, fast, and pray concerning our hearts or simply address the situation openly with the person who offended you. James 5:16 says, "*Confess your faults one to another, and pray one for another, that ye may be healed. The effectual fervent prayer of a righteous man availeth much*" (KJV).

Getting rid of a root of bitterness and dealing with chronic anger is a process. It is a significant remodeling project, where it isn't enough to just put some paint on your walls. God is going to have to demo the walls, expose the problem to His light, and then rebuild your life without that septic poison.

Jeremiah 1:10 says, *"See, I have this day set you over the nations and over the kingdoms, to root out and to pull down, to destroy and to throw down, to build and to plant."* God wants to root out and pull down your bitter root and destroy and throw down the pride, anger, and bitterness that built up around your life. Only when He has removed the old pain, the old hurt, and the clinging bitterness can He begin to rebuild your life.

The good news is that there is nowhere you can go that's beyond His help. You are never so far gone that He cannot help you if you will surrender it all to Him. His plans for you haven't changed. Later in Jeremiah the Lord says, *"For I know the thoughts that I think toward you, says the Lord, thoughts of peace and not of evil, to give you a future and a hope"* (Jeremiah 29:11). He said this to His people who would be in exile and to whom a bright future probably seemed far more impossible than how you see your own future.

Pray this with me: "Father, I pray for the areas where I have directed anger towards others in my life or held anger inside of me. I ask that You forgive me and take all the anger away. Heal my heart, Lord, and take away any infliction from my words and actions towards others and myself. Holy Spirit, I ask that You help me to speak sweet words of healing. In Jesus' name, Amen."

Whatever the cause of your bitter root, do not let it stay in place one more moment than necessary. Take action—get help. Talk to a counselor, your pastor, or another qualified person who loves the Lord. But determine today to take the first step toward freedom.

The Consequences of Anger

If you don't deal with your anger, whatever types you experience, you will eventually develop a bitter root, and the consequences are grave. The angry person ends up alone, embittered, and miserable, and this lifestyle brings with it obvious consequences but also some that may surprise you.

No one really wants to be around an angry person, so anger is destructive to your relationships, and eventually you will find yourself isolated—by your own actions and choices and at no fault of those who've left you alone. You drive them away with your anger. Proverbs 21:19 says, "*Better to dwell in the wilderness, than with a contentious and angry woman,*" but this is as true for men as women. People just don't like being around angry people.

Not only will you be increasingly alone, you also will be more subject to health problems if you do not deal with your anger. Some of the short- and long-term health problems that have been linked to unmanaged anger include:

- Headache
- Digestion problems, such as abdominal pain
- Insomnia
- Increased anxiety
- Depression
- High blood pressure
- Skin problems, such as eczema
- Heart attack

Isolated people tend to get depressed, and the anger (which is often at ourselves at some level) makes us not even really want to be with ourselves. Depression is a natural result of feeling like this.

Is your anger something you can afford *not* to address? How many of these problems do you need in your life before you take action? We can let the problems stack up until we're ready to snap, but I hope that you will act sooner—before a bitter root, depression, or any of these health problems impact you or your family too gravely.

Anger and the Family

An angry, depressed person is a drain on a family. When we give place to these emotions and let them run us, we drag our families down and can turn relationships toxic.

A friend's wife is now able to see how her mother and father's anger at one another poisoned their family. Married at an early age, they quickly grew to apparently hate one another. Her mother was domineering, loud, and obnoxious, and her father was quarrelsome, controlling, and bitter. He withdrew from the family, and when he would try to weigh in when he couldn't handle something anymore, he did so angrily. Abuse followed, with correction turning overly physical, especially with the older boy. The eldest daughter escaped through alcohol and relationships with men, the two sons turned to drugs, and my friend's wife rebelled, ironically, by turning to Jesus. Though this husband and wife stayed together, their anger at one another poisoned their family, and the toxic environment continues to reproduce itself in the lives of three of their children, including the loss of one son to an overdose and the incarceration of the other on drug-related charges.

Harboring anger in your heart is like adding poison into your family's food. It brings toxic sickness that grows over time, building up in the systems of each family member until it reaches a critical point. When it finally reaches a point where their emotional systems cannot process it, the sickness that may have been hard to detect until that point suddenly manifests in terrible and destructive ways. People do unwise, unhealthy things, relationships strain and break, and the sickness becomes obvious. The disease can simmer just under the surface of an apparently fine family, but at the heart is a cancerous growth of anger and bitterness.

Much of anger's power to destroy is made possible because of this secrecy. People deny it is a problem, and it is allowed to fester in the dark. If we could communicate about it, uncovering the problem and exposing it to the light of God's Word, we would rob anger of much of its destructive power.

One show on TV I especially liked while growing up demonstrated how a father could interact with his wife and children. He cared about his family, and his approach inspired open communication. When one of them was angry and acting out, he cared enough about them to want to know why. If there was a problem, he didn't let it fester—he searched it out and brought it into the open. I modeled my own policy of openness on this approach and pursued communication in my family that is open and transparent.

When I am mad, I tell them. When they are mad, I want to know why. We get it out in the open, exposing it to the light. In the dark, anger grows; exposed to light and truth, it tends to whither. Remember, often we get angry when we don't yet have all the facts, and we can quickly fix that by simply getting everything out and communicating openly. There's no excuse for letting misunderstandings create long-standing anger when you could simply clear it up.

Angry Kids

Our kids learn anger from us—they learn how we handle it and what to do with it from how we do it. They mimic what they see. If they see you harboring anger against your spouse, fuming and foaming over something he or she has done, that is what they will mimic. If they see you explode to get your way, that is what they will do. But if they see you process it like a rational, Spirit-filled follower of Christ, full of grace because you've been shown grace, that's how they'll behave too.

If your child is showing anger problems, start the solution by looking at, and addressing, your own anger problems. Then you can start working with your child's anger issues. The same principles in this book will help them as well.

I have counseled with angry kids, and I always look to the parents for what they've modeled to their children. One young man I saw for years grew up to go to college and was an A student, but his dad was not involved in his life, and you could tell that he was hurt and angry. He was quiet about it, but if you knew what to look for, you knew there was a furnace in there somewhere. When we got down to it, he did not understand why his father had not been there like he was supposed to be.

His mother was angry over how things had gone in their lives. Her response to the events in their lives has been to hover over him, and he felt she was on "ten" all the time—she's always on high alert, always on the edge, and with no margin. She is probably a great example of overwhelmed anger. If something deserved a response that's at level three, she was already at ten—or even eleven! As he got older, this young man would then go to eleven right with her, escalating to match her.

This young man has done much better, and I was glad to see him head off to get a college degree. However, I've seen angry kids turn to the streets. They are hurt and disappointed with how things have gone in their lives, they're angry at perhaps a dad who left, a mom who's strung out, and how unfair life is, so they run with the wrong crowd and find an outlet in being somebody else. I believe that much of the trouble with our youth is anger. They're angry that their fathers aren't home, that their homes are chaotic, and that they feel like they don't have options and no one cares. So they turn to the streets, and they violently vent their anger at each other.

Other kids turn to sex or drugs. How many pregnant young girls end up that way because in addition to their need to be loved, they're angry, and they're acting out by being with boys as a way of striking back? They look for love in the wrong places, and they don't know it, but they're setting themselves up to perpetuate a cycle of disappointment, anger, and bitterness.

The best solution for the parent with the angry child is to start dealing with it early. Learn to look for warning signs like these:

- My child blames others for his or her troubles.
- My child throws or breaks things whenever he or she feels frustrated or irritated.

- My child changes the rules of games when playing with other children.
- My child is stubborn and refuses to do what he or she is told to do unless you use the right tone of voice or approach.

The same things that hurt you also hurt them, so if you've gone through trauma as a family, be aware that the pain can turn to anger in your children just like anyone else.

Talk to your children. Whatever age they are, and however far along they are in their own anger journey, talk to them. Be present, and give them your full attention. Be honest, and don't keep secrets or play games with them. Be vulnerable about your own frustrations and concerns, and urge them to do the same, even if they don't want to. When they do talk, listen attentively, don't interrupt, and above all else, *don't go off on them!*

I talk to many parents who don't know how to apologize. Maybe they think they don't have to apologize to their kids, but consider this: You are teaching them the forgiveness process by demonstrating it to them. You make mistakes, just like they do, so let them see how to handle it when you mess up and need forgiveness. Model repentance and forgiveness for them.

I've had to do it plenty of times. You might tell them, "Hey, I shouldn't have yelled. I shouldn't have lost my temper. I was wrong. Can you forgive me?" There are plenty of times that you can be right in your parenting but go about it the wrong way, such as in anger. You might be correcting a problem, but if you become a problem yourself, you have something to make right with them. It doesn't let them off the hook; it just means you have to keep your own rules. Don't try to get them to keep a different standard than the one to which you hold yourself.

Let your children see you work on your own anger. Invite them into the process. Teach them what you learn, and be quick to confess your faults and failures to them. You may think you need to project confidence and authority, but they will thank you for modeling honesty and repentance and a willingness to work on your problems far more than they will respect you for being aloof and superior. Show them how we should handle difficult emotions like anger by letting them see you do it. I'm not saying you cry on them and be a mess; just be honest with what you are feeling, and include them instead of trying to keep it from them. Trust me, they know even if you think you are keeping it a secret.

You do not have to be perfect, so let them see that you've come to terms with that and you are working to get better—for them and for yourself.

I see parents who are angry with their kids, and almost every time, they are seeing things in their children that they have in their own lives just reflected back at them. If you see it in them, chances are excellent you played a role in putting it there. That is not a condemnation or accusation; it is a reminder that you need to extend mercy to them like it has been extended to you. If they're making you mad, you need to be extra intentional about keeping your cool and demonstrating mercy and forgiveness to them. Work your tools, and let them see you on the journey.

When they see the difference in you, it will make them thirsty to experience it for themselves. Working on your anger issues is a deposit for the future—both for yourself and for your children.

If there has been a cycle of anger and abuse in your family, decide that it ends with you. This is the end of the line! Tell the enemy he can't have your family, because you are taking anger away from him as a weapon to use against you! The cycle ends now, with your decisions and actions, and you have the opportunity to replace it with a tradition of godliness, thankfulness, forgiveness, and humility.

Matthew 18:18 says, *"Assuredly, I say to you, whatever you bind on earth will be bound in heaven, and whatever you loose on earth will be loosed in heaven."*

It is time to break the chains over yourself and your family.

8
THE ANGER ACTION STEP

Most people know what our issues are. We just don't want to admit or confront them.

The alcoholic knows he drinks; the drug addict knows she does drugs. The promiscuous person knows he sleeps around. They just won't face their problem. We want to get better, even if we can't admit it.

If you are still reading this book, it is either because you know you have an anger problem or have someone in your life who does. Until you come to terms with your anger problem and take action, you are giving anger a foothold in your life.

It is time to decide if you are going to do something about it or not.

If you don't, if you choose to continue down this road, your problem is only going to get worse. It will get further entrenched and more a part of your life. The devil's foothold will grow until you have a root of bitterness and chronic anger poisoning your life, driving away everyone you love. If you don't act, you will be increasingly isolated until you are alone—and you won't like your company any more than anyone else does. Depression, regret, and health challenges will follow, until anger has stolen your entire life from you.

But that is not the way it has to be. You can choose to look anger in the face and tell it that it will no longer drive your life. You can take your life back from this emotion that once promised you control but instead took it from you.

It will come out, sooner or later. But you can deal with your demons publicly when your anger slips out, or you can deal with them between you and the Lord and the tools He's shown me for this book.

If you are willing, you can heal. If you are willing, you can regain the foothold the enemy has taken. You can learn to deal with your anger God's way, and you can be restored from the toxic bitter root that has been poisoning your life and your family.

If you do, God has amazing promises He's eager for you to experience.

Getting rid of your anger leaves room in your life for something else—something better. God has a good future in mind for you, and He wants you to walk in His blessing.

The First Step: Decide

Many times, we're waiting to *feel* something before we *do* something. We want to feel like forgiving before we forgive. We want to feel brave before we risk. We want to feel loved before we give love.

But often a key to life is *deciding* and *doing* before we have the *feeling*. We decide to forgive even when we're still offended. We decide to be brave while we're still scared, and we decide to give love before we know if it will be returned.

We *decide*, then we *do*.

You want to no longer feel angry before you deal with your anger problem. You may want the situation to change, the people to ask for forgiveness, or the hurt to heal, but the first step to dealing with your anger is to decide to let it go. Either you will manage your anger, or it will manage you.

If a desire for control has been driving your anger, it is time to let go of the idea that you can control everything. It is time to put your trust in God and to stop trying to work the situation around to what you want it to be. We will discuss pride in depth in a later chapter, but it is pride to think that you know better than God, so it is time to surrender your pride and accept that for now this is where God has you.

Can you trust Him enough to see you through whatever situation you are in, even if you don't like it? Can you trust Him in the middle of your fiery furnace? Can you trust Him even in the wilderness? Will you be still and know that He is God? Or will you kick against the goads and willfully resist whatever it is He may be trying to teach you while you are here?

It is your decision.

You can decide to stay where you are...and be angry about it. Or you can decide to trust God and deal with the problem through *thankfulness*.

Yes, thankfulness!

If hurt is behind your anger, it is time to accept that your pain has an expiration date. The Bible tells us not to let the sun go down while you are still angry—in other words, your anger has a time limit. Your pain has an expiration date. And if you choose to hold onto it beyond the healthy period for grieving, you will be clutching poison to yourself.

So, will you cling to something poisonous? Or will you choose to let it go and accept the blessing of the Lord in its place? Even if you've been wounded, wronged, and sinned against, will you let it go? Will you set the prisoner of your anger free? If so, you will find that *you* were the prisoner, not the person who sinned against you. Will you trust God enough to make things right in His way? Will you trust Him to heal you in His timing? Or will you make your pain and hurt your identity and slowly let it poison everything good in your life?

It is your decision.

You can decide to stay in your pain, wallowing in it...and poisoned by it. Or you can trust God to deal with the problem His way by choosing to *forgive*.

We've identified the problem. Whatever kind of anger you have, you are angry. It was probably once justified. Something drove you to this anger, and for however long now, anger has been in the driver's seat of your life. But it is time to take leadership of your life away from this emotion that can lead to sin and replace it with your redeemed, born-again, blood-bought spirit.

You do that, first and foremost, by making a choice right now, this very moment. This is a pivotal time for you, because you either decide here and now you are going to do this, or you decide to stay subject to your anger, its consequences, and the enemy of your soul who is using it as a foothold to gain influence and control of your life.

Which will it be? Set down this book and choose now, but I urge you to do this: choose life.

Choose Life

I am going to trust the Lord that you chose to lay down your anger and replace it with the blessing of the Lord. I'm glad you did, because you chose life.

God gives us tests in life, but He also gives us the solutions on the test: He tells you which to choose. He spelled it out to Israel in Deuteronomy 28:2-13, which I encourage you to read for yourself. He described every way in which He would bless His people for obeying Him. After explaining it, He then put them to the point of decision as I just did you, and He said this:

> *I call heaven and earth as witnesses today against you, that I have set before you life and death, blessing and cursing;*

therefore choose life, that both you and your descendants may live; that you may love the Lord your God, that you may obey His voice, and that you may cling to Him, for He is your life and the length of your days; and that you may dwell in the land which the Lord swore to your fathers, to Abraham, Isaac, and Jacob, to give them (Deuteronomy 30:19-20).

You have chosen to handle your anger God's way, and in so doing, you've chosen *life*. That choice will result in the blessing of God, and you will never regret having chosen life throughout the length of your days. Like Israel, you will be blessed in the city and the country, blessed while working, and blessed while resting. You'll be blessed when you go in and when you go out, because you have chosen the path that leads to life.

You cannot experience any of these blessings on your own or by your own effort. You cannot be blessed or saved by keeping the law, because that's impossible, for we are sinful humans. Instead, we must rely on Jesus Christ. If you ask Him, God will give you life, help, and healing, and this is what will allow you to deal with your anger His way—He will give you the power to do so by giving you His most precious gift, *Himself*. The power that raised Christ from a borrowed grave lives in you, my friend, and it is that life-giving power that will allow you to exchange anger for grace, hurt for forgiveness, and control for thankfulness.

The power to handle anger God's way stems from our identity in Christ. We are all, at the very foundation of who we are, children of God. Before anything else, and more important than anything else, is our identity in Christ Jesus, who bought and paid for us. Because of Him, we can live a godly life. Because of His tools and His Holy Spirit within us, we can do it God's way. Without that power, we cannot do any better than "managing" our anger the world's way.

Our jobs may come and go, friends and loved ones may betray us, and our situations may change; and all these things may make us angry. But if you identify yourself as a son or daughter of God, a joint-heir with Christ Jesus our Lord, your *identity* will never change. And because of that, you can have faith in God that He will never leave you or forsake you, He will always be with you, and He will always meet your every need—including the one that has driven you to anger.

Dealing with your anger God's way starts with recognizing your position in Christ, and understanding that Jesus knows exactly where you are at. We do not have a High Priest who cannot sympathize with us; we have one who understands our situations and our frame. He faced everything we do—all the pain, the betrayal, the frustration, the injustice, and all the rest—yet He did not sin. In fact, He was occasionally angry, but He did not let it get control over Him by letting it become sin. Whatever has made you angry, Jesus can understand it.

But He didn't stay angry. He forgave. He had mercy. He pursued justice and healing, but He did not sin, and He did not let anger or frustration or anything else drive Him. His Spirit was in the driver's seat, doing whatever the Father told Him to do. You, too, can have your redeemed spirit in the driver's seat of your life, and we're going to spend most of the rest of this book talking about how to do that.

Steps for Dealing with Anger

We have already talked about the first step in dealing with anger: a decision to choose life. You cannot do all the right things, so you ask God for His help, and from there you can begin to take His path to dealing with anger. Let's now take a few moments to look at the other steps we'll be going over in the next section of the book.

Practice Forgiveness

The second step to dealing with your anger involves recognizing that people are just human. The same mistakes that they made two thousand years ago are the same ones they make today. Jesus taught us what to do about this as He was being crucified: "*Father, **forgive** them, for they do not know what they do*" (Luke 23:34, emphasis added).

People are just people. They do things that hurt us. But because of our identity in Christ as new creations filled with His Spirit, we can choose to *forgive*. If you've been hurt, you can choose to receive His healing. If you are frustrated, you can choose thankfulness. And somehow, in a way that transcends human understanding, these choices for life take on a power of godliness that will *change our lives*.

This does not mean that we forget and expose ourselves to toxicity and danger. It does not mean that we roll over and let people continue to hurt us. It does not mean we continue to smash our heads against the wall. We get to safety, we receive His healing, and we humbly allow God to order our steps. But we also forgive those who have hurt us, and we let go of the offenses that seek to entrap us.

You may find it interesting to know that one of the words for offense used in the Bible is the same word for the little stick that props up a trap. When we buy into offense instead of forgiving, we are trapping ourselves. When you choose to give in to anger, it is a trap. But forgiveness is the key to releasing yourself.

We can forgive because we recognize that people are just people, and they all make mistakes. If you are honest with yourself, you've made a mistake or two in your life; so have I. It frees you up when you understand that other people make them too, and just as you want grace when you've messed up, you must in turn give grace to those who have messed you up.

You can choose to let their mistake bind you up in the trap of offense, or you can choose to forgive and learn from it.

A Lifestyle of Thankfulness

The next step God taught me is *thankfulness*. After you ask God for help and begin to forgive, we let thankfulness replace our desire for control and the frustration that comes when we realize we do not have that control. We humble ourselves and surrender our pride, choosing to thank God for His blessing upon us.

God became frustrated with the children of Israel for their bitter complaining and unthankful attitude in the wilderness. Throughout Scripture, we learn that God desires a thankful heart, not a bitter, complaining one.

As long as we are angry and worked up that we have not gotten our way, we are living with an unthankful attitude, and so the key to dealing with that is to choose thankfulness as actively as we choose to forgive. Again, you will not feel like it—you are not waiting to *feel* thankful before you choose to *be* thankful. You cannot be angry and willfully want your own way and thankful at the same time, for one will drive out the other. So, you must choose to be thankful.

Learn from Your Mistakes

Next, I believe that we are to learn from our mistakes. God hasn't given us a mind and then told us not to use it; He wants us to learn and grow and mature. So, I believe that as we make our choices to forgive and to be thankful, we also ask the Holy Spirit for wisdom to make right choices in the future.

Like David, we ask the Holy Spirit to search our hearts and show us where there is any wicked way. I call this taking a spiritual inventory. We use our minds to look at our actions and choices with the wisdom and discernment of the Holy Spirit, and then take it a step further and consider how we can prevent ourselves from making the same mistakes again. We all make mistakes, but we do not have to make them over and over—we do not have to make a *lifestyle* out of a sinful mistake. God does not want you to stay there, friend, and He will be with you as you develop a plan for growing past that hang-up, weakness, or tendency toward sin.

I believe God wants us to be active in taking action steps to move away from sin. If you are angered by viewing social media, get rid of it. Jesus tells us that it is better to cut off a hand or eye if it will keep you from sinning; cutting off social media is a small price to pay for removing a source of anger in your life. Create action steps that will help you to not sin in your anger, and then, with the help of the Holy Spirit, do them.

Move On

Finally, we must move on. It is time for you to quit bringing it up to yourself. If you've genuinely repented to God and you've received His forgiveness, you must also forgive yourself. You are not holier for holding yourself in a penalty box or punishing yourself, thinking that is how you show repentance. You do not show God how serious you are about repentance by beating yourself up. That is more than counter-productive; it is actually *unbiblical*. It is pride to hold yourself in unforgiveness when God has called you forgiven. It is time to quit beating yourself up for what you've done and accept His forgiveness and move forward.

The Bible tells us that when we have asked for forgiveness, God no longer remembers our sin. He has removed our transgressions from us as far as the east is from the west, and He remembers them no more (see Psalm 103:12).

In the context of the Lord's Prayer, Jesus says this: "*But if you refuse to forgive others, your Father will not forgive your sins*" (Matthew 6:15 NLT). This is why it is so incredibly important for you to forgive others. You must forgive if you wish to be forgiven, but if you are repentant and you are forgiving others, you have done your part in receiving God's forgiveness.

You must forgive yourself and let it go. You must choose to see your past mistakes like God sees them—under the blood of Jesus Christ (which means He sees them no more and no longer holds them against you or even remembers them). It is your turn now to decide to accept God's forgiveness and to *act like* you are forgiven.

Let it go. Even if others do not, in your heart, you must move on. Read what Jesus told the woman caught in the very act of adultery in John 8:10-11: "*When Jesus had raised Himself up and saw no one but the woman, He said to her, 'Woman, where are those accusers of yours? Has no one condemned you?' She said, 'No one, Lord.' And Jesus said to her, 'Neither do I condemn you; go and sin no more.'*"

That is Jesus' response to your sin: *You are forgiven.*

Those around you may not act as the woman's accusers did and leave you alone, but you must know the truth in your heart. That truth is this: "*There is therefore now no condemnation to those who are in Christ Jesus, who do not walk according to the flesh, but according to the Spirit*" (Romans 8:1).

If Jesus calls you forgiven, can you come into agreement with Him? Can you choose to be thankful to God, even when your circumstances are sour and difficult? Are you ready to learn from your mistakes and forgive yourself? If so, you are ready to begin taking the steps that will deliver your life from a stronghold of anger.

We read, "*No, dear brothers and sisters, I have not achieved it, but I focus on this one thing: Forgetting the past and looking forward to what lies ahead, I press on to reach the end of the race and receive the heavenly prize for which God, through Christ Jesus, is calling us*" (Philippians 3:13-14 NLT).

Like Paul, I do not claim to have finished my race yet. But I am here to urge you on and to teach you the things God taught me. And if you've read this far, you have chosen life and chosen blessing. So let us take the next steps in this journey together by taking an in-depth look at the two most important components of dealing with your anger. In fact, they are so vital, I have dedicated a chapter to each of them: forgiveness and thankfulness. We will begin by exploring what it means to practice forgiveness.

9
THE PRACTICE OF FORGIVENESS

In the previous chapter, you took your first step to dealing with your anger problem by making a decision. You have chosen life and to deal with anger God's way. No longer is it in the driver's seat; you are choosing to have your spirit firmly in charge of your life.

You may be wondering what comes next. I believe that the next thing we must do as we deal with our anger is to get right with God. We do this through repentance and forgiveness.

We learn the practice of forgiveness.

A few years ago, our church was outgrowing our current building. We wanted to buy a new location. A local church was going through foreclosure, and it was due for an "absolute" auction. It was absolutely going to be auctioned, so if you bid on it, you were required to buy it. We got the bank approval necessary to buy this building, went to the auction, and won it. We thought we had our new building!

However, after we won the auction some people involved did things behind the scenes that were like a stay of execution on their foreclosure. They kept delaying it and delaying it, although the auction had required that it be sold to us. It began to get messy and unethical, and there were violations for which we could have sued. Not only that, we'd had to produce hundreds of thousands of dollars at the auction, and we were meeting the financial obligations on our end, which extended our church financially. It was an uncomfortable position to put our church in.

We were getting ready to pursue legal action when one member of my congregation asked me a very good question: "Where in the Bible is it that you should sue another church?"

I believe in acting and living according to God's Word, and I could not answer him with a biblical basis for what we were about to do.

I had let my emotions get caught up in this whole thing, and I realized I was very angry about how it was being handled. These were Christians not acting like Christians, but now I was getting ready to do something that was also not biblical—because I was angry at what they were doing.

I realized that though I couldn't ignore what was going on, I needed to forgive. And, I didn't need to act unbiblically myself just because they were. I called our attorney and told them we were going to drop the suit and not file or take it to court.

He told me that we were nearly obligated, in order to get our money back, to sue them. In fact, by *not* suing them, we could expose ourselves to consequences as though we had not made good on our part of the auction's obligations. In the worst-case scenario, we could lose our money—hundreds of thousands of dollars—and still not have the building we needed.

I told him, "I believe that if we do what is right, God is going to honor it." He couldn't believe it, and I had to talk to him for a week before he finally listened to me. We didn't file the suit, and our attorney told the court we were backing out of the deal, which we weren't supposed to do because of the structure of the auction.

However, we were determined that our church would act according to God's Word and that we would pursue a lifestyle of forgiveness not just as individuals but as a church body. We laid it before God in prayer, and we trusted that if we would do it His way and let this go, He would take care of us.

And He did! A couple of weeks later, the escrow company that was holding our money agreed to let us get it back.

We act and behave according to God's Word, not according to how we feel. We choose to forgive and do things God's way, even when it seems we may have repercussions in the Word for it.

I tell you this because you may be thinking that anger and forgiveness only work in the terms of relationships. But the principle of forgiveness is in every aspect of our lives, and it is a key to the prison of offense that can leave us bound and trapped.

I know that this story seems insignificant if you have been badly hurt, and it is not my intention to liken us forgiving a church with whatever hurt you may have experienced. Remember, comparison is not the path God gives us.

Instead, I hope you see through this that the need for forgiveness is everywhere within our lives. The invitation to sin through anger will come up, even at church, and it is my desire that you learn how to deal with it God's way. Forgiveness isn't a one-time event; it is a *lifestyle*. So, let us look at forgiveness together and see how it is God's plan for you to let go and let Him work in your life.

Practicing Forgiveness

You will have trouble with anger if you do not practice a lifestyle of forgiveness.

When I say "practice" in this sense, I mean it like a physician. Doctors are never *done* with medicine; they practice it continually.

Forgiveness is not just forgiving for a specific offense; it is learning and practicing a lifestyle based on God's principle of forgiveness. There will always be something new to forgive.

I think we all know that we're *supposed* to forgive, but we make up excuses about forgiving. Some people say that whatever hurt them is so much greater than what other people forgive and that they simply cannot do it—it is too big. They compare their heart to others and they decide they're exempt from forgiving those who hurt them because their hurt is greater or bigger or special. Some precious people have been deeply hurt, betrayed, and wounded, and they will point out that emotionally it is very, very difficult—even impossible—to forgive when you have been badly wounded. They are correct.

Others claim that things don't bother them, and they live in denial instead of forgiveness. They think they're being longsuffering, but what they're really doing is pretending it doesn't bother them...in hopes that it won't. But it doesn't work that way. They think they're being un-Christian to be hurt or offended by things, so they hide it—even from themselves. Thus, they don't deal with it God's way.

Both kinds of people—and every other kind of person who does not wish to let go of hurt and offenses—must learn to forgive God's way. There are many reasons we do not forgive, but there is a massive problem if we do not, which I mentioned in the previous chapter:

If we do not forgive, we *cannot* be forgiven.

You Must Forgive If You Want to be Forgiven

If you want to get right with God by being forgiven for your own sins, including anger, start by forgiving others. Paul tells us, *"Make allowance for each other's faults, and forgive anyone who offends you. Remember, the Lord forgave you, so you must forgive others"* (Colossians 3:13 NLT).

Now, carefully read Jesus' instructions to us about forgiveness in the Lord's Prayer, starting with verse 12:

> *And forgive us our debts, as **we have forgiven** our debtors [letting go of both the wrong and the resentment] ... For if you forgive others their trespasses [their reckless and willful sins], your heavenly Father will also forgive you. But if you do not forgive others [nurturing your hurt and anger with the result that it interferes with your relationship with God], then your Father will not forgive your trespasses.* (Matthew 6:12,14-15 AMP, emphasis added)

Look at verse 12 again. The language here implies that we are asking God for forgiveness *after* we have forgiven others.

The Son of God states it with crystal clarity that if we forgive those who sin against us, our Heavenly Father will forgive us. And if we do not forgive, we will not be forgiven.

This is difficult to accept. It seems unfair in a way, or perhaps legalistic. As you let that sink in, you may be saying to yourself, "But, Pastor, you don't know what he did to me," or, "I've been hurt too many times, and I can't let it go."

It seems humanly impossible to let go of and forgive those who have wounded us most deeply. And it is. It is impossible—for man. However, *"With men this is impossible, but with God all things are possible"* (Matthew 19:26).

I am going to teach you how to forgive God's way, and you will see that it is not about your feelings or performance but about God's power and love acting in you and through you. With His help, it *is* possible—even when you have been badly hurt—though it may not look exactly like you thought it would.

Your decision to forgive is the key to the prison of anger that is holding you bound to your pain and anger. Will you use it to free yourself?

How to Forgive

Most people try to use their feelings to forgive people, and they use their feelings as a barometer for how successful they are at forgiving. If they feel better about someone, they think that means they can forgive that person. If they're still angry or hurt, they do not forgive. The same way, we feel like we've truly forgiven someone when we no longer feel strongly negative anymore.

The problem is, you may *never* feel better about that person. That person may never be good, or safe, or loveable. You may never feel like forgiving, and if you wait to feel it before you do it, you could be waiting forever. And in the meantime, as we read from Jesus' own words, your unforgiveness is preventing your own sins from being forgiven.

Of paramount importance in learning to forgive God's way is accepting that forgiveness is a *choice*, not a feeling. We choose to forgive *because God said so.* Is that hard? Yes...if you think you must do it alone, on your own power.

But we are not asked to *feel better* about someone who has hurt us; we're simply told to make a decision to live in forgiveness instead of unforgiveness. The decision comes first; the feeling may come later...or not at all. The feelings are unnecessary; the decision is completely vital. Your feelings can catch up later.

Forgiveness isn't what you feel in your heart or think with your mind. Forgiveness is what you decide with your spirit and say with your mouth. We read in Matthew 9:2, "*Then behold, they brought to Him a paralytic lying on a bed. When Jesus saw their faith, He said to the paralytic, 'Son, be of good cheer; your sins are forgiven you.'*" Jesus *spoke* it—and it was this forgiveness that set this paralyzed man free. A few verses later, Jesus says, "*'So I will prove to you that the Son of Man has the authority on earth to forgive sins.' Then Jesus turned to the paralyzed man and said, 'Stand up, pick up your mat, and go home!' And the man jumped up and went home!*" (Matthew 9:6-7 NLT).

Jesus spoke forgiveness with His words. This man received what he needed—healing—when forgiveness set him free. When you speak forgiveness with your mouth, *you* are set free to be forgiven. Your words are the precursor to what your body will experience. We confess with our mouths, then believe in our hearts (see Romans 10:9).

It Is About "Love" Not "Like"

Biblical forgiveness does not require that you like someone. It does not require that you be around that person. It does not require that you allow that person to abuse you or continue abusing you. We are required to love everybody—yes, even *that* person—and forgive them. But we are not required to keep getting hurt. You can love someone with God's *agape* love from a distance, because God tells you to, without exposing yourself to further injury from them.

It may help to think about it like this. I like going to Washington Wizard basketball games, and I could be in an arena with literally thousands of other people. When the Wizards score, I may stand up and high-five the guy next to me, and we may celebrate together, but that doesn't mean we're friends. It doesn't mean I *like* him. It means we have something in common, and we can lay down whatever differences we have during the game to come together for a like purpose.

So too, when we are in Christ, we are family, and you don't get to choose your family! But you must love them. We are to be united in vision and in Christ, we are all running the same race, and we are on the same team. That doesn't mean we're all best friends; you may hardly be able to stand another believer. But they will know we are Christians by our *love*.

So how do you actually *do* this? You ask God for help. You decide with your mind to obey God's Word and forgive, and you execute it with your mouth in faith that God is going to honor your conscious choice to forgive, even when you do not feel like it.

You must constantly ask God for His help to love and forgive, for without Him, we can do nothing; but with Him, we can do all things! You may not ever feel like it, but you can still obey through the power of the Holy Spirit. And you may have to give that person to God in forgiveness daily, even hourly. Every time the hurt flares up, you may need to make the choice again and speak it out. You keep doing this, asking God for help, until the fact of your feelings begin to catch up with the truth of God's Word.

Eventually, the pain decreases. You may never like this person, but God will draw off the infection, the toxic wound within you, and the pain will decrease. In its place, He will give you peace.

Receiving Forgiveness

Because you are choosing to practice forgiveness like a doctor practicing medicine, you will also be in the practice of receiving forgiveness. We get right by God through accepting Jesus, but we stay in right relationship regarding forgiveness by continually forgiving those who sin against us so that we may receive His forgiveness in turn and walk in His peace.

Peace is one of the benefits God has in store for you in exchange for your anger. It is part of the blessing of the Lord. One of the ways we get peace is triggered by forgiveness. It opens the door and allows the peace of God to come settle on you.

We have talked about forgiving others, but if you are dealing with an anger problem, you likely need to ask for forgiveness *from* others, too. You forgive that you may be forgiven.

The first, of course, is to ask God to forgive you. This is part of the repentance process. Remember, repentance means more than being sorry—it means turning away from whatever you've done and turning back to God. Thankfully, as we've discussed, God is slow to anger and quick to forgive, and while His anger lasts for a moment, His favor lasts a lifetime. He promises to forgive us if we will humble ourselves and repent, and His Word is full of instances where He allows circumstances to draw His people to repentance. Whatever you have gone through or are going through, let it draw you to repentance.

We read in 1 John 1:9, "*If we confess our sins, He is faithful and just to forgive us our sins and to cleanse us from all unrighteousness.*" But then we must also confess our sins to one another (see James 5:16). That means that if you have sinned against others in your anger, you must seek forgiveness from them as well.

Anger damages relationships, so this is where you begin to help others heal. You show these people that you are truly repentant through your actions, not just your statements. Ask them to forgive you. Apologize to those who have been affected by your anger with genuine humility. No fake apologies or dancing around the topic; own up to it that you've hurt them, no matter your justifications, and ask them how you can help make it right through restitution. Match your actions with your words.

But do not be too surprised if those you've hurt take a while to forgive. Now is not the time to preach to them, and it is certainly counter-productive to get angry with them for not forgiving you right away! Give them time and space. Remember, we prove our change through our fruit. In time, they will see the good fruit of the change God is working in you, and relationships will begin to be restored.

Restoration is a process. Relationship was not broken overnight, and fixing it will not happen instantly either. As you show them you've changed, God will mend what anger has broken.

Now, do not be confused; guilt is not your ally in this process. There is no condemnation to those who are in Christ Jesus (see Romans 8:1), so any feelings of guilt and condemnation you have in this are not from God but from your enemy, the devil. Condemnation attacks your character and worth, and it is from the enemy. Conviction tells you an action, thought, or belief was wrong; condemnation says you are a bad person. Conviction is the sure, direct, and specific correction of God regarding specific parts of your life out of line with His Word. Conviction brings godly repentance and restoration.

God calls you the righteousness of God in Christ Jesus (see 2 Corinthians 5:21). God calls you holy. God calls you His child. *That* is your identity—not a person of guilt and condemnation. You are not an angry man or woman, a sinner, or an awful person. You are a blood-bought child of God, and He paid the ultimate price for you to be restored to right relationship with Him. Because of Jesus, you were restored to God, and through practicing forgiveness you can be forgiven.

It Is Time to Forgive

In the last chapter, I urged you to make your decision and choose to deal with your anger issue. Now it is time to take the next step. I want you to sit down and prayerfully ask God whom you need to forgive.

Pray this with me: "God, please examine my heart and show me everyone I am holding in unforgiveness. If I am holding anger or bitterness against anyone, please tell me."

Get out a pen and paper or your phone, and write down whatever He tells you. Linger over this as long as it takes, and after God has shown you a few names, pray something along these lines over each person individually: "Lord, I choose to forgive. I let go of my anger, bitterness, and pain regarding [INSERT THE PERSON'S NAME], and I choose to forgive them because that is what Your Word says to do. I know Your Word will not return void, and it says that as I forgive others, You also forgive me. Thank You for Your forgiveness."

Do this as often as necessary. You'll know it's necessary because when you think of someone, you are filled with anger or another negative emotion. Whenever you feel that way, forgive them again and give it to God, asking for His help. Eventually, your heart will begin to catch up with the decision your spirit has made. Until then, do something like this often...and watch as the list of names begins to shrink and the venom against these people diminishes over time as God works His healing.

You likely have others to whom you are apologizing. Pray that they forgive you. It may be good to make a similar list of those you've hurt and to pray for them daily. Pray that they learn to walk in forgiveness, as you are. Keep praying and trusting God, but remember—it is *your* job to forgive *others*, and it is *their* job to forgive *you*.

As you practice forgiveness and as you ask for forgiveness from others, God will work healing within you and in your relationships. Anger may have caused hurt and damage, but God is the great Healer, and when you do things His way, His Word says that He is faithful to forgive and to cleanse you from all unrighteousness. Your decision to forgive begins this process, your words execute it, and you will start to see the results of doing it God's way over time. It *will* happen. As surely as the rain comes down from Heaven and waters the earth, producing good fruit, His Word *never* returns void in your life (see Isaiah 55:10-11).

Forgiveness is the key.

10
THE PRINCIPLE OF THANKFULNESS

The practice of forgiveness helps you make things right with God and others, but it is the principle of thankfulness that diffuses your anger and helps keep you free. Thankfulness is an antidote for the poison of anger and is a powerful tool for preventing your anger from becoming sin.

Thankfulness is simply choosing, no matter what is going on around you, to be thankful to God for everything He has given to you and done for you. Thankfulness, like forgiveness, is a lifestyle—it is a practice that is to be part of our daily lives—and it sets the stage for changing your life from one of anger and bitterness to one of humility and gratitude.

It is very hard to be angry and thankful at the same time. The two are simply incompatible. If you tend toward anger and *do not* choose thankfulness, your default will be anger, frustration, and eventually bitterness. However, if you intentionally choose thankfulness, you can short-circuit your anger before it has a chance to develop into sin. If we wait to feel like being thankful, as with forgiveness, we can be waiting a long time, so again we see that the principle of thankfulness is a *choice*, not a feeling.

We cultivate thankfulness by stopping and being mindful of what God has given to us and done for us. There are endless ways to recognize God for who He is, what He does, and how He loves us that will inspire thanksgiving within us. It is an act of humility to be thankful to God even in the middle of difficult situations, but that is exactly what God has called us to do.

Always Give Thanks

The Word is filled with instructions to give thanks to God. David wrote one of the most well known: *"Enter his gates with thanksgiving; go into his courts with praise. Give thanks to him and praise his name"* (Psalm 100:4 NLT).

Yet God steps it up when He tells us to be thankful *in all things* through Paul's words: *"Be thankful in all circumstances, for this is God's will for you who belong to Christ Jesus"* (1 Thessalonians 5:18 NLT).

That seems like a tall order, doesn't it? In *all* things? Surely God doesn't expect you to be thankful when people are treating you poorly. What about when your job is in jeopardy—or you just lost it? Or when your relationships are crumbling? Would God expect you to be thankful to Him even after someone has hurt you?

The answer is yes: We are told to give thanks no matter what is going on.

How are we to do that? How are we supposed to be thankful during *any* circumstance—even the bad ones? Again, the key to this is that we cannot do this on our own. It is just not sustainable. I have met thankful people who did not know Jesus, but maintaining a lifestyle of thankfulness is a function of the Holy Spirit within us placing our spirits in the driver's seat.

There's always something to be thankful for. A recent news story serves a good example of this. A University of Virginia student was wrongly and improperly arrested for something he didn't do, and it inflamed racial tensions locally and was part of a bigger picture of anger bubbling just under the surface at a national level. I choose to use this ugly situation as an example of how we can be thankful in any situation.

I told my congregation that they could start by being thankful that this young man wasn't killed, which has often been the story lately. I told them we can be thankful that this situation hasn't happened to their son or daughter. We can be thankful that there was a cell phone video of what happened. We can be thankful that the media gave this story attention, helping hold the authorities accountable for their actions. We can be thankful that some have stood up to say that this isn't right, and so on. There are always reasons to be thankful—if we will look for them.

Now, I want to clarify something: The Word tells us to be thankful *in* all things; it does not tell us to be thankful *for* all things. There are some who believe this way, but I do not think our loving Father puts us in bad situations and then demands that we're thankful for them. However, He can *use* any situation and work it for our good (see Romans 8:28). He can teach us through any situation, good or bad, and He will certainly not waste anything.

We live in a fallen world under the temporary rule of the enemy, and bad things happen to good people. But good things also happen to bad people, and our Father causes it to rain on the just and unjust alike—we all have something for which to be thankful.

Even in a situation that rightfully makes you angry, you can find things to be thankful for because you know that God is always with you and He works all things to your good. This is an excellent way to diffuse your anger before it becomes sin.

Thankfulness Produces Peace

Thankfulness reduces anger because it brings peace. Think about it: If you believe God is in control and can be trusted enough that you can be thankful no matter what is going on, how does it affect you? Trusting God like that produces peace in your heart. Peace, like thankfulness, precludes anger—you can't be peaceful and angry at the same time.

We are able to participate in godly thankfulness when we let the peace of God, which surpasses our understanding, guard our hearts and minds (see Philippians 4:7). Peace can rule our days instead of anger or worry. We read, *"And let the peace that comes from Christ rule in your hearts. For as members of one body you are called to live in peace. And always be thankful"* (Colossians 3:15 NLT).

If you let your thoughts focus on those things that make you angry, your anger will grow, because you are feeding it. If you, instead, choose thankfulness and peace, you will feed them and starve that fire of its fuel. Paul puts it like this: *"Finally, brethren, whatever things are true, whatever things are noble, whatever things are just, whatever things are pure, whatever things are lovely, whatever things are of good report, if there is any virtue and if there is anything praiseworthy—meditate on these things"* (Philippians 4:8).

Choosing to focus on these things, like choosing to bring all your concerns to God in prayer, produces peace, because it aligns your thinking and helps create an attitude of gratitude. Anger requires fuel, and contrary to what the world thinks, you do not fight fire with fire. If you encounter a situation that makes you angry, you do not deal with it in a godly way by fueling it with angry thoughts. Instead, you embrace the opposite spirit—that of thankfulness. It is like putting water on a fire instead of pouring gas on top of it.

You can choose to fuel your anger, or you can choose to fuel peace. Which do you want in your life? You get to choose.

The next time you are confronted with an opportunity to be angry, I challenge you to do this: Look for something to be thankful for. When someone cuts you off in traffic, thank God that you didn't get in a wreck. If you do get in a wreck, thank God for insurance, or seat belts, or hospitals. There is always something for which to be thankful, and thankfulness will produce peace in your life and rob anger of its fuel.

The Most Thankful People on Earth

Living a lifestyle of thankfulness is not easy to do—it is impossible! But if it is impossible, how does God expect us to do it? Because you don't do this by yourself. On your own, it is impossible. But with God, all things are possible for you. The power to practice thankfulness is the same resource for grace, forgiveness, and love: God's never-ending supply. God never runs short, and when His Holy Spirit is living in you, you have a direct connection to the same power that resurrected the Lord Jesus. You are not doing this alone, nor should you even try.

Because of this unending supply of God's power in our lives, I believe Christians should be the most thankful people on earth. If we truly trusted God to be faithful no matter the situation, we could honestly thank Him in all things, no matter what, because of our faith.

So how do you start becoming one of the most thankful people on earth? I believe it often starts with the little things. If you are in a dark, bitter place, you may not feel like you have a great deal to be thankful for. But I would challenge you that if you dig deeply enough, you can find something for which to be grateful at any time of your life.

Earlier I mentioned thanking God because you weren't in an accident. But perhaps it needs to be even more basic than that: Did you have breath this morning? You can be thankful for that. Were you able to get out of bed this morning? Some cannot do so; you can be thankful for that. Could you be thankful for the job you don't like because you realize there are others who would be thankful for any job at all? Could you be thankful that you have two legs to walk? Eyes that see? Ears that hear? Yes, any of these things can fail us, but at any given time, we have much to be thankful for.

In fact, if you live in the United States of America, as I do, we have so much to be thankful for it is absolutely ridiculous. According to a report, "Many Americans who are classified as 'poor' by the U.S. government would be middle income globally, according to a new Pew Research Center analysis."[1] The report stated that more than half of Americans are "high income" according to the global standard, and only 2-3 percent are low income or "poor." Do you have a car—any car at all? If so, you are among the richest people in the *world*. If you make minimum wage, you are making many times more money than half the people in the world today. If you have more than one pair of shoes, more than one set of clothes, and a bed to sleep in, you are materially blessed, and you have much to be thankful for. There are likely *billions* who would gladly trade places with you right this moment.

Jesus tells us, "*If you are faithful in little things, you will be faithful in large ones. But if you are dishonest in little things, you won't be honest with greater responsibilities*" (Luke 16:10 NLT). So, be thankful for the little things, and show yourself faithful with them. Sometimes your thankfulness must start small, so start intentionally looking in your life for little things you can be grateful for. If it starts with your shoes and works up, that's okay!

---

[1] http://www.pewresearch.org/fact-tank/2015/07/09/how-americans-compare-with-the-global-middle-class/

Practice Thankfulness

Thankfulness requires practice. We live in a dissatisfied culture that is always focused on the next thing, not on what it already has, so being thankful is often counter to the theme of our culture. But I guarantee that as you practice it with little things, you will find opportunities to be thankful for bigger ones.

Luke tells a story from Jesus' ministry. As Jesus went to Jerusalem, He passed through Samaria and Galilee, and there ten people with leprosy saw Him and called to Him from a distance. They could not come close because of their disease, but they wanted to be healed.

> *And they lifted up their voices and said, "Jesus, Master, have mercy on us!" So when He saw them, He said to them, "Go, show yourselves to the priests." And so it was that as they went, they were cleansed. And* **one** *of them, when he saw that he was healed, returned, and with a loud voice glorified God, and fell down on his face at His feet, giving Him thanks. And he was a Samaritan. So Jesus answered and said, "Were there not ten cleansed? But where are the nine? Were there not any found who returned to give glory to God except this foreigner?" And He said to him, "Arise, go your way. Your faith has made you well"* (Luke 17:13-19, emphasis added).

These people were desperate for healing; there was no medical hope for them, and their condition separated them from everyone they loved. They needed a big miracle from God, and Jesus had mercy on them. Yet, though ten were healed, only one of them—a despised foreigner from an apostate land—came back to thank Him.

How often are we among the nine rather than the one who stops to thank God? How often has the Lord blessed us, and we simply went our way without thanking Him? This was a big thing—healing—but we are blessed *daily*, and all too often we do not make a point to thank God for His blessing.

Let this be a new season for you—a season of thankfulness. Let this spur you to remember the blessings that God has given to you. If that is difficult, start small. If life is hard right now, trust me, it could always be worse. So thank Him for what you *do* have.

You're reading this book because you want help with anger, so why not start thanking God *now* for the healing that He is ministering to your life? Be like that Samaritan who returned to thank Jesus. And think on this:

All ten were healed of their leprosy. Yet in the *King James Version*, we read that Jesus told the one who returned, "*Arise, go thy way: thy faith hath made thee **whole***" (Luke 17:19, emphasis added). People with leprosy lose fingers and toes, the end of their noses, and suffer other damage to their extremities. Is it possible that while the others were healed of their disease, this man who returned to thank Jesus was made *whole*?

The Bible does not clearly say, but I will tell you this with confidence: it is always better to be thankful than not. You never lose anything with gratitude, but you can gain a great deal. A better attitude and a way of diffusing anger are powerful benefits to embracing the practice of thankfulness.

The Power of Appreciation

Appreciation is thankfulness expressed outwardly. It is a chance to show we're thankful, so a practical step to increasing in thankfulness is to be appreciative to others. Show it when you are at the store, getting something to eat, or with friends. You can impact people one at a time, so make it a mission to show your appreciation to each person you encounter in your life. Show genuine appreciation to the sales clerk at the store, to the server at the restaurant, to the usher at church. You're establishing a lifestyle of being thankful *as life happens*—not waiting to thank God for it at the end of the day, but as it happens.

Thank God through praise and worship. Humble yourself and praise Him; let His praise continually be on your lips. I dare you to try to stay angry when you are lifting your hands in praise to God for five minutes! It is impossible to stay angry while focusing on praising God. Sing Him songs, pray without ceasing, and simply spend time appreciating His presence without saying a word. Bring your thankful attitude to church with you. A thankful attitude can change the atmosphere. Just like a grumpy, angry attitude can change the tone of the room for the worse, so a grateful one can change it for the better. Your choice for thankfulness can change the room.

James writes, *"Every good gift and every perfect gift is from above, and comes down from the Father of lights, with whom there is no variation or shadow of turning"* (James 1:17). Everything we have comes from Him, and He is the Father of *light*, not darkness— of good, not evil. Whatever is good in your life, you owe it to God.

I have met people who are angry with God, and dealing with that starts here: recognizing that God is good, all the time, and that everything you have comes from Him. If it is good, it is from Him. And even if it doesn't seem good, He is so full of love that He *works it* for your good! When you begin intentionally thanking God for things, you will find it increasingly hard to be angry with Him.

This is true for any relationship. If you will look for things to be thankful for in your spouse, you will begin to find more. If you will look for things for which you are thankful in your children, your job, and your life, you will find more and more of them. And as you thank God for them, and show them your appreciation, you will find it diffusing your anger toward them.

The Love of God

Appreciation is just another form of love. We read, *"Now hope does not disappoint, because the love of God has been poured out in our hearts by the Holy Spirit who was given to us"* (Romans 5:5). When your hope is in what someone does, when they do not do what you want, you get frustrated. You get angry. But if your hope is in the *agape* love that the Holy Spirit has *already* poured into your heart, you aren't putting your hope in what they *do*. You're putting your hope in *who God is* in them. This hope will not lead to disappointment, and then that disappointment will not lead to anger. You can always be thankful for God's *agape* love, because it is unconditional and not dependent on others doing what you want. You can just be thankful for them and love them.

Thankfulness lets that love God has poured into your heart flow out. It is a way of expressing it. You can let it be tied up because you are angry, or you can love anybody, no matter what, in any situation, because it is not your love—it is God's love. And this love of God will smother your anger, because thankfulness is an expression of love, and love is a remedy for anger.

As I have said, there are times certain people are unsafe; I get that. But be careful about building walls and keeping your love in. We think we build walls to protect us and keep bad things out, but walls go both ways—they keep things in, too. God wants your thankfulness and love to flow out of you to Him and to others, and you can dam it up and stop the flow with unforgiveness and being unthankful. Instead, set it free, and watch God work through His love spread abroad through your heart.

Start Today

With forgiveness, I asked you to make a list of those you need to forgive and people who may need to forgive you. Today, we are going to start a thankful journal.

Sit down ready to write things out. Pray and thank God for the help of His Holy Spirit in making you more thankful, and then begin to write some things for which you are grateful. Start small if you want and build up. No matter what, you have *something* to be thankful for, so begin wherever you must, however small it may be. Do not despise the day of small beginnings; just start. Write something—*anything*!

I suggest making a practice of writing down a few things every day. Force yourself to do it. There is something special and powerful about writing it out—especially when you are down and depressed, at which point you can bring out your list to remind yourself what God has done. Every time you get blessed, write it down, because you may need the reminder later. Keep doing this until it becomes a habit, and let the attitude of gratitude transform your thinking.

Thankfulness is an incredibly powerful tool for dealing with anger because it diffuses it and brings peace. Forgiveness sets you free; thankfulness keeps you free. If you want freedom from anger's grip over you, this is how you get it and keep it. It is time to transform your life with the principle of thankfulness.

11
MORE PRACTICAL STEPS TO DEALING WITH ANGER

In chapter eight, we talked about the practical steps for dealing with anger: recognizing you have it, choosing to do something about it, practicing forgiveness, the principle of thankfulness, learning from your mistakes, and moving on. Forgiveness and thankfulness were so important, we spent the last two chapters discussing them in more detail. Now I want to cover a few other practical ways that God showed me for dealing with our anger as well as some ways of implementing these things into your life.

Slow Down

Earlier in the book, I mentioned that anger often occurs in a state of ignorance—we often get angry when we do not yet have all the facts. When we rush to judgment, we can easily be mistaken. Proverbs 18:13 says, *"Spouting off before listening to the facts is both shameful and foolish"* (NLT).

God is slow to get angry, and we are called to be like Him. Notice the emphasis I put on certain words in these scriptures. The Psalmist writes, *"The Lord is gracious and full of compassion, **slow** to anger* *and great in mercy"* (Psalm 145:8). James builds on this in the New Testament by writing, *"So then, my beloved brethren, let every man be **swift** to hear, **slow** to speak, **slow** to wrath; for the wrath of man does not produce the righteousness of God"* (James 1:19-20).

One great way to slow down your anger is to stop to assess the situation. Don't jump to conclusions. As I mentioned earlier in the book, asking questions is a great way to clarify what really happened and get some understanding. Some things are outright affronts against us—disobedience, defiance, intentional slights and insults—but you could be misunderstanding something. Or, instead of an intentional action, what you are about to get angry about could just be an accident or mistake. The response appropriate for a deliberate attack is different than an accident. You won't know until you slow down long enough to assess the situation.

Most of us have been quick to get angry with a spouse or a child. I remember a time after God had started working with me on my anger when my son had done something that really set me off. I had been practicing being calm, so I slowed down, chose my words carefully, and listened to his explanation. Come to find out, he did not do what I thought, and I was so proud of myself for not losing it. Praise God, this stuff really works!

What level of response is appropriate for what really happened? Earlier in the book I mentioned a young man who had anger just bubbling under the surface of his life, and one reason was that his mother was always on "ten." No matter what was going on, her response was a level ten, and that means it was often inappropriate for the level of offense. He may have made a mistake that should have been a "three"—a minor irritation. But instead, she flew off the handle at the slightest thing because she had no margin and did not give herself time to respond. If you react to everything like you are starting World War III, people are going to get tired of you!

Be slow to anger, and take the time to assess what's really going on. Then, evaluate what a proper response is. If you are hungry, angry, lonely, or tired, HALT—just *stop!* Don't trust yourself to respond. If it is your kids, tell them you will be dealing with it later—they're not off the hook, but you can wait until you have a clearer perspective to respond rightly. Very few situations demand that you respond instantly; most times, you can afford to give yourself some time to get all the facts, get yourself under control, and then respond appropriately to the true level of the situation.

Commit to trying one of these things today, and then work on using each of these practices during the week:

1. **Slow Down**—Take a moment before you respond, and get away from the situation if you need to in order to have a thought-out, well-measured response to the situation.

2. **Assess What's Really Going On**—Ask questions and get all the facts so you can form a logical response. Don't let the first wind of emotion drive you; use your brain.

3. **Respond Appropriately**—Measure your response to the offense. Ask the Lord for help in reacting with wisdom.

The Greater One Is in You

At times, we can just feel out of control. Anger can flare up in an instant, and if you experience fits of rage, you can feel like you have lost control. Afterward, you may recognize it and feel badly, and you may wonder how you are going to keep it together. If you are a born-again believer, this is how you are going to start keeping it together: After writing about the powers of this world and its current ruler, John writes, *"You are of God, little children, and have overcome them, because He who is in you is greater than he who is in the world"* (1 John 4:4). You have the Greater One living on the inside of you!

Instead of claiming that you are out of control or that you lose control, I want you to start confessing, "I am not out of control, because the Greater One lives inside of me. The fruit of the Spirit produces self-control in me." God is always in control, and His Spirit lives within you—the fruit of Him within you is love, joy, peace, patience, kindness, goodness, and *self-control* (see Galatians 5:22-23). You do not have a spirit of fear or any other ungodly thing like anger; you have a spirit of power, love, and self-control (see 2 Timothy 1:7). There is nothing you cannot handle, and you can respond to any situation in a godly way without losing control—not because of you but because of the One living in you.

Realize that these things are true and practice speaking them over yourself. Choose one to confess over your life today, but learn all three and begin to claim them for yourself:

1. **The Greater One Lives Within You**—Remember whose you are. He who is in you is greater than he who is in this world (see 1 John 4:4).

2. **Your Spirit Is in Charge**—You are under no obligation to do what your fleshly nature urges you to do (see Romans 8:12).

3. **The Spirit Produces Self-Control**—The Spirit of God lives within you, and a by-product of His presence includes self-control (see 2 Timothy 1:7).

You Have Help

The next point I want to make is related to the last one that the Greater One lives within you. Because of that, you are not left to do things by yourself. You have help. Not only is the Greater One on the inside of you if you are born again, but you have help from the Holy Spirit. The Holy Spirit ministry is to help us. He is called "The Helper," and most of us miss the ministry of the Holy Spirit because we never ask Him to help us.

God knows you cannot do this on your own, and He has not asked you to. If you could change yourself, you would've done it already! If you could sanctify yourself, you would not need Him in you! But He knows you need Him, and He has provided a Helper.

Jesus said, "*I will pray the Father, and He will give you another Helper, that He may abide with you forever*" (John 14:16). He sent that Helper on Pentecost, and believers have had access to Him ever since. He helps us in our weakness (see Romans 8:26).

Pray and ask Him for His help. "Holy Spirit, help me keep my tongue in check. Help me with my anger." Or you might pray, "Holy Spirit, I messed up; would You forgive me and help me make it right?"

I've had conversations with Him like that. There are times I didn't want to apologize, but He helped me do the right thing. On my own, I wanted to be *right*. I wanted to stay in my pride and have it *my way*, but He helped me to humble myself instead of exalting myself.

My conversations with the Holy Spirit went from, "Help me make it right," to "Catch me before I do it!" I got tired of living my life as a janitor, always cleaning up messes. If you will slow down, you will give the Holy Spirit time to work on you and ensure you are responding with your spirit in the driver's seat. If you are tired of cleaning up messes, ask the Holy Spirit to get out in front of that thing, and then be open and listening for Him when He tries to warn you away from doing something you shouldn't.

You would expect that with any other sin—you'd expect the Holy Spirit to convict you before you stole something, or before you lied to your boss, or before you cheated on your spouse. Why would we not expect Him to warn us before we sinned with our anger? You can no longer claim you are out of control, because your *spirit* is in control, and you are not driven by your fleshly nature any longer. You who are children of God are now led by the Spirit of God, not by your sinful nature (see Romans 8:14).

Pray and ask God for one of these things frequently this week, but move toward the third one—asking Him to help prevent you from sinning in your anger.

1. **Ask the Holy Spirit for Reminders of His Presence**—He is always with you, but we do not always feel His presence (see Matthew 28:20). You're not on your own, so cultivate the awareness of the Holy Spirit.

2. **Ask the Holy Spirit for Help**—He is the Helper, and He is ready to help you with everything pertaining to life and godliness (see 2 Peter 1:3).

3. **Ask for Help Before You Sin**—Ask the Holy Spirit to keep you from sinning, not just to help you pick up the pieces after you do (see Jude 1:24).

Show Love

When we talked about thankfulness, I mentioned the power of God's love to transform your anger. Experiencing that love is powerful, but it is like forgiveness—it is best when given away.

If you find yourself angry a lot, here is a practical act that will help you: go out and do nice things for other people. Show them love. Give things away. We all have a few clothes in our closet that we are just not going to ever get back into; grab some and give them away. Don't have a yard sale; find those who need things, and give them away. Give money if you have it, time if you don't. Showing God's love to others by giving is a powerful antidote for anger. You can be thankful because you are blessed, so now it is time to turn around and be a blessing to others.

What are some things you could do *right now* to give to others? First of all, you do not have to give large amounts of money; a small amount with the right spirit to the right person can be far more meaningful than big sums. Do not despise the small things; after all, Jesus pointed out that a widow's two pennies were more than any rich person gave:

> *While Jesus was in the Temple, he watched the rich people drop-ping their gifts in the collection box. Then a poor widow came by and dropped in two small coins. "I tell you the truth," Jesus said, "this poor widow has given more than all the rest of them. For they have given a tiny part of their surplus, but she, poor as she is, has given everything she has"* (Luke 21:1-4 NLT).

You may have money you can give, and that is wonderful, but what do you do if you do not have enough money to give beyond your tithe? Does this technique not apply to you? No, I believe it does, because what do we exchange for money in this economy? Our *time*. Our *knowledge*. Our *ability*. Do you have time you could give? You could volunteer at church and give that way. Do you have knowledge you could give? You could help educate another or do something for which you are uniquely qualified. Perhaps you have ability. Maybe you are good with your hands and at making things, or you can fix a car, or you can hem a dress. There are many ways you can give with your time, knowledge, and ability that will change lives and will *get your eyes off yourself.*

Again, it is not about the amount—it is about your heart. Jesus is after heart change, and He can do a great deal of that when you give cheerfully. Paul writes, "*He who sows sparingly will also reap spar-ingly, and he who sows bountifully will also reap bountifully. So let each one give as he purposes in his heart, not grudgingly or of necessity; for God loves a cheerful giver*" (2 Corinthians 9:6-7).

It is important to show the love of God to other people—partly because of how annoying, frustrating, and imperfect they are—but you also diffuse anger by showing love to God. I mentioned earlier that it is nearly impossible to stay angry after even just five minutes of genuine praise to God. Raise your hands, close your eyes, and let go of all the things of this world that are trying to hold you down. Lose yourself in simply praising your God!

You can praise and worship Him in many ways, and you do not need to wait for church. You can sing along with music and others worshiping in your car, your home, or nearly anywhere else, thanks to mobile devices and headphones. The best thing is that you can even do it in public (though you may want to sing in your spirit rather than out loud when you are at McDonalds).

If you are feeling angry, you can excuse yourself, go to the bathroom, and praise God in a quiet song, through scripture, or even in your prayer language. Your praise does not even need words!

Pick one of these things to do right away, and then make time to do it—in the right spirit. Then in the next two weeks, find a way to show your faith by doing each of these things: serving, giving, and praising, and watch how God uses these things to diffuse your anger.

1. **Find a Way to Serve Someone Else**—A humble heart that is serving someone else makes a poor environment for anger (see Galatians 5:13).

2. **Give Something Away**—Giving is an antidote for many temptations of this world, including anger. Remember, you don't have to give money (2 Corinthians 9:6-7).

3. **Praise God**—At church or alone, use praise as an antidote for anger. You can praise the Lord any time you feel tempted to anger (see Psalm 34:1).

I hope these things have been helpful to you. You may benefit from making a list out of each of the challenges I suggested: slowing down, remembering God is with you, asking the Holy Spirit for help, and showing love. Then, intentionally work on them as practical treatments for your anger.

These have been practical steps for dealing with your anger. Now, in the next chapter I want to talk about the anger battle that takes place on a different field: the battlefield of the mind and your imagination.

12

VAIN IMAGINATION

At the beginning of the book, I mentioned the definition of anger: "strong feeling of intense displeasure, hostility or indignation as a result of real or imagined threats, insults, frustration, or injustice towards yourself or others." I want to focus in on a specific portion of this—the role imagination plays in anger.

We have talked extensively about getting all the facts before you allow yourself to be angry, but I want to take that a step further. Because sometimes we get angry and it isn't just because we lack the facts—we actually *make stuff up* that is not true, and it is that imagined stuff that has made us angry.

As I mentioned earlier a woman once threatened to leave my church because she believed that another woman, among a congregation of hundreds, was staring at her from across the room. She was so angered by this that she brought it to my attention and angrily told me she was leaving the church because of this other woman. She was offended and had many venomous things to say about the woman she felt had been staring at her.

I didn't want to get involved, but I wanted to put down discord in my church, so I asked this other woman about it. Not only had she not been staring, she had no idea this angry woman even existed! The entire thing, including all the negative things the woman who was angry had described, was all in her imagination. She had imagined that insults were directed toward her when none were, and it was enough for her to fly off the handle and want to leave the church. Because she was so angry, this woman was moving herself out of the place where she was being blessed, and I believe this is an excellent illustration of what can happen when we let our imagination create anger within us.

Imagination Run Wild

God is an imaginative God. Just look at all the animals! Only someone of endless creativity could have made them. We, in turn, are created in His image. Our ability to imagine what is not and then help make it come to exist is powerful and modeled after our Creator's own power to imagine and create. However, just as this imagination He has given us can be used to great good and His glory, it can also get us into trouble.

I believe that a great deal of the things that make us angry are not just from not having all the facts—they are "vain imaginations," often inspired by our enemy himself just to sow discord and get the people of God to move out of the place where they've been receiving blessing.

We are instructed in 2 Corinthians 10:5 to cast down *"imaginations, and every high thing that exalteth itself against the knowledge of God, and bringing into captivity every thought to the obedience of Christ"* (KJV). These are the proud, rebellious thoughts, and they are a product of two things: the lies of the enemy and the self-focused excesses of our own imaginations. These imaginations are not the good kind; they're the kind where our anger fantasies run away with us. Those are the kind of imaginations we are to bring into captivity and teach to obey Christ.

Has your spouse or a friend ever done something that you didn't like and then you constructed an entire story in your mind, almost instantly, about how that person did it on *purpose* to hurt you? Has someone ever dropped an innocuous comment, and you immediately began wondering what they *really* meant by that? We can do it almost without thinking, and it is a vain imagination.

Perhaps your wife didn't get the *one item* that you added to the grocery list when she went to the store. It is fattening, and you are trying to watch your diet, and you jump to the conclusion that she is insulting you because of your weight—all without saying a word to you. She just didn't buy that thing at the store. But by the time you see her next, you are already hot—you are angry, and you've been insulted even though she never said a word.

Or maybe your husband fails to comment on a new outfit or article of clothing or an accessory you thought made you especially beautiful. You're headed out to dinner, and you've gotten all dressed up to impress him and remind him of what it was like when you were newlyweds, but he didn't even notice—or worse, *doesn't like*—that new item you thought set the outfit off just right! It goes from not noticing to not liking, or maybe even to him thinking you spend too much. He never said a word, which is bad enough, but now he's "*saying something*" with his silence—and you are *mad!* You went to all the effort to get dressed up, and *he* doesn't like it and thinks you spend too much! You storm out the door, ready to give him a taste of his own medicine at dinner, and he hasn't said a thing.

This narrative can happen in any relationship: spouses, friends, coworkers, extended family. We can imagine the worst in others so easily (yet of course expect that others give us the benefit of the doubt). This is a vain imagining—which puts you at the center of a story that is hurting or insulting to you...but *does not even exist.*

Yet imaginary or not, you get *mad.* And not only that, you can sometimes cling to your angry story line and nurse those hurt feelings even when the truth comes out.

Maybe your wife was exhausted from a long day when she went shopping, and she got distracted by a text from one of your children and just forgot your item. Your husband wasn't intentionally ignoring your new item or making a comment about your spending habits; he's just a man and didn't notice that special touch or he had a bad day at work. But you are already mad when you find out the truth— and maybe you want to stay mad because it is easier than admitting the whole thing was in your head. It is easier than humbling yourself, apologizing for your anger, and accepting that your little anger fantasy was actually *wrong*.

Has this ever happened to you? Come on, be honest! How often have fights or arguments or resentments started in ways just like this?

The details of the anger fantasies have infinite variety, but the source is the same: a vain imagination. We build a fictitious world where we are the victim, the wronged person, and the other person is the bad guy. But you do not need to live in a world of prideful, imaginative anger. We're going to talk about dealing with these, and it starts with being healed of your own insecurities, which the enemy preys upon when he joyfully helps us create these anger fantasies.

Unhealed Insecurities

At the heart of most vain imaginations are insecurities. We often respond with anger in areas where we are insecure or hurt. They are weak places in our lives, so like a wounded animal, we'll bite and claw and fight to protect that hurt place if we even *think* someone may be getting too close to it. We can think others see the same flaws we see in ourselves, or that they're magnifying them, and it can make us very angry very quickly. It is a defense mechanism.

You may be riding home from your wife's sister's house and comment that she made some good meatloaf. What your wife heard was, "I don't like your cooking," when all you meant to do was give her sister a compliment. A vulnerable spot got exposed, and you now must spend some time assuring her that you love her cooking, hoping you don't end up eating ramen noodles the rest of the week. Thank God you didn't compliment her sister on losing some weight!

You may comment to your husband that he should spend more time with your son. What your husband heard was, "You're not a very good father," when you simply meant to convey to him that your son is having a hard time in school and could use some extra attention. Now you are trying to sooth his wounded pride and gruff manner.

The issue wasn't what you *said*, it is what was *heard*. Because of insecurity, your comments get transformed into something else because they get caught up in a vain imagination. You may not even know that is what triggered it, but your angry conversation may not even be about the topic—it could be about a vain imagination that threatens an unhealed insecurity.

A friend of mine talks about getting angry with his wife during the summers because she and their daughter stay up later and later when he still needs to go to bed so he can get up for work. This cuts into their time together as a couple and when my friend feels his attempts at showing leadership through a more structured bedtime are unsupported, he gets angry because he feels his wife does not want to spend time with him. In truth, it has little to do with not wanting to spend time together and has far more to do with it being light out later, getting up too late when not on a school schedule, and unhealed emotional hurts both husband and wife received during some medical crisis in the recent past. While he understands that this is largely a creation of his own imagination, the feelings are hard to shake, and he finds himself frustrated and irritated by them. Have you ever experienced something like this?

A great deal of the trouble with these vain imaginings happens when we *interpret* someone else's words or actions and read into them. We look between the lines, and we come away with conclusions based more on our own inner demons than what the person said, did, or meant. We have all been guilty of this, but not everyone gets as *angry* as someone with an anger issue. If you have an anger problem, these vain imaginings can be very hard on your relationships and a point of contention within your home.

Does staying up late mean someone doesn't want to spend time with you? Does complimenting someone else's cooking mean they do not like yours? If you are dealing with insecurities, wounds, or reading into these things, they become triggers for our angry flare-ups, but the truth was that none of those things was *true*.

Expose It to the Light

When the reaction is not justified by the action, it is a "trigger." I mentioned before that some people are just on "ten"—they're perpetually reacting too strongly to every little thing. To someone else, not commenting on an outfit would create no great reaction; but to you, it is inflammatory. To someone else, forgetting something at the store is just forgetfulness; to you, it is an intentional slight. To someone else, staying up late is just par for the course for summer; to you, it is a marriage crisis. Any of these things may be a "one" or "two" in the right context; in *your* context, your overreaction is not justified.

One of the first things in dealing with these vain imaginations is to ask ourselves if that person is normally like what we're accusing them of being in our minds. Do they often mock us? Criticize us? Slight us? If we gave them the benefit of the doubt, what level of response would their action justify? Is their offense a "one" or a "two," but we're treating it like an "eight"? Is our reaction really justified?

We cannot see this clearly if we lack the right perspective. We need the light of truth to shine on these things.

Have you ever gotten dressed in the dark and then found that your outfit or socks don't match because you couldn't see properly?

I have walked out of the house with one black and one blue sock because I was looking at things in the wrong light.

The first step in casting down these vain imaginations is to get in the right light—the light of truth. The proper light is the light of the Word and learning to see others and ourselves as God sees us. The Bible calls us children of the light, and when we're in the dark, we are going to get hurt. We are people of the light, not the darkness, and when your vain imaginations develop in the dark, they are going to lead to injuries.

There is only one true, clear light, friend. That is the Word of God. The Word, Jesus, is the light of the world (see John 8:12), and when He is in us, He calls *us* the light of the world (see Matthew 5:14). We are bearers of His light, but it all starts with the truth of the Word of God.

To cast down a vain imagination, expose it to the light of the Word. What does the Word say about the insecurities behind your angry triggers? Does God say you are below and beneath, or that you are above and more than a conqueror? Does He say you don't have enough, or that your Father owns the cattle on a thousand hills?

The truth is, Jesus makes up for any perceived insufficiencies you may feel you have. The truth is, Jesus made you the head not the tail, above only and not beneath. You have no need to feel inadequate and defensive, because you have everything you need through Him. It is not up to your spouse, your children, your boss, your coworkers, or any other human being. They do not have that kind of power over you, so don't give it to them!

His grace is sufficient for you—and it is sufficient for the person your vain imagination has vilified, too. As you have freely received, what would happen if you freely gave? What would happen if you recognized that truth about yourself as stated by God, and then you extended the same grace He gave you to others?

You would be very difficult to hurt and offend; you would no longer have your weak places and vulnerabilities because you'd let Jesus heal them. You would not give place to anger fantasies or vain imaginations. Now, I'm not saying this happens overnight, but it is a process that can begin now and will rob vain imaginations of the weaknesses they prey on.

Earlier in the book, I told you that a practical way to deal with anger is to expose it to the truth. Nowhere is this as true as it is for vain imaginations—when exposed to the proper light, they literally fall apart. Start with exposing them to the Word of God, and then I dare you to set your anger and imagination aside and open up to the person who is "making you mad."

You definitely want to get the whole picture, which can involve asking questions like we've talked about before, but also try this: Humbly tell them what's in your head. Expose that lie—let's call it what it is—to the open air, and dare to find out if it is the truth.

Ask her, "Honey, are you saying I'm fat? Is that why you didn't get me the large bag of pork rinds I put on the list?" You'll find out she just got distracted—or she wants the whole family to eat healthier and didn't buy a few other things you normally get at the store.

"Do you not like my outfit? Are you saying I spend too much?" you might ask your husband. And he may tell you that he didn't notice it because of some very troubling things that happened at work.

Ask her, "Do you not want to spend time together? Do you not prioritize our marriage? Is that why we don't get our daughter in bed at a reasonable time?" She may respond, "I didn't realize you felt that way. Let's set a more realistic time to talk while our schedule is crazy this summer."

Ask him, "Do you think I'm a bad cook?" Or ask her, "Do you think I'm a bad father?" Then listen as you get the truth. Then, take it one step further: Ask God. "Father, do You feel this way about me?

Is this true?" and wait for an answer. God will shine the light of His truth. Are you willing to receive it?

Don't Do Life Alone

If you will dare to expose your lie to the light, you can get help casting down your vain imagining. You weren't designed to do life alone; you were designed to have people in your life who can tell it to you straight. They aren't there to tell you what you want to hear; they are there because they love you enough to tell you the *truth*. And you give them permission—and encouragement—to do it!

Your spouse should be one of these people. He or she should have the right, which you explicitly give, to pull you back down from the ledge where your vain imagination takes you. And you need to *listen!* Husbands, listen to your wives! God put them in your life to bless you, and they are a "good thing." She's there to help ground you, help you process your emotions, and connect you socially to your family and friends. She has certain skills and sees some things more clearly than you do. Listen to her!

Wives, listen to your husbands. God created him to be strong and to protect your family, and he has certain skills and sees some things more clearly than you do. Listen to him! In your love for one another, desire the best for each other. Submit to one another. Be willing to sacrifice for each other, putting yourselves second and them ahead of you. You need their perspective.

I have used the example of an Indy car crash in my church. I showed how the footage from one car made it look like this other car caused the accident. The footage from another made it seem like a different car caused the wreck. However, the footage from the blimp overhead showed a completely different result—it was that third perspective that was clearer. On the track, you are too close to the action, and you need people in your life who can provide that outside perspective.

And then—and this is key—you must accept what they have to say. You must listen to them. Your spouse is in your life, partly to tell you truth. They're often very different than you are, and that is a good thing! Your differences can make you stronger! You must be willing to listen—to have chosen in advance to hear them.

Philippians 2:3 says, "*Let nothing be done through selfish ambition or conceit, but in lowliness of mind let each esteem others better than himself.*" Who do you esteem that highly? Who has that right in your life to speak to you and bring you down from your ledge? Who are you submitted to, who can hold you accountable and give you a clear perspective you've chosen, in advance, to trust?

Your mate should be the chief one, but accountability partners and good, trusted Christian friends should be on this list. Your pastor should be on it. These are people you've chosen to trust before there is a crisis and you've reacted to a vain imagination.

So, what if your spouse is your excuse for your anger? Maybe you don't trust him or her because you've been hurt. We don't have space to make this a marriage book in addition to an anger book, but I will say this: Begin approaching your marriage using the tools I'm giving you in this book.

You can transform that relationship by dealing with *your* anger. Is your spouse a part of the issue? Very probably. But you cannot change him or her; you can, however, change *you*. With God's help, you can deal with your own anger, and then when you've taken your half out of the equation, you can deal with the troubles in your relationship easier because your own big triggers are out of the picture or you at least know how to process them.

Forgiveness, thankfulness, and all the rest are powerful tools. Also, *remember prayer*—pray actively for your spouse. Pray for restoration in that relationship, and make it a cornerstone for your practices of forgiveness and thankfulness. It is very hard to be angry with someone you are actively forgiving and being thankful for.

God can restore intimacy to your marriage, and intimacy is a cure for insecurity. Removing insecurities takes the fuel out of many vain imaginations. Some people think intimacy is just sex, but that is just a small sliver of what intimacy means. Think of it like this: "into me see"—intimacy.

You must be vulnerable with your spouse to get the most benefit out of this. Men especially struggle with this. Men, let her see into you. Draw her out like you did when you were dating; listen to her. She loves you! Women, when he does so, do not dare use it against him. Honor it when he tries. Know that while he may be physically stronger, in this area he may likely be the weaker one.

When you are both committed to loving Jesus and loving each other, you will not use those vulnerabilities against each other—you will use them to *heal* one another! That is a big purpose God has in marriage; through this relationship, which models Him and the Church, you get healing. You can be a big part in bringing healing to your spouse.

Typically, no one can make you angry like your spouse can. But the same potential to make us angry is also true for healing: No one can help bring healing like your mate can! God desires to use your spouse to help tether you to earth and reel you back in when you get carried away.

Give someone you trust the right to speak truth into you today. If you are not married, find a person of the same sex who is godly and trustworthy, and pursue vulnerability and honesty. Give that person permission to rein you in, and trust that they're acting in your best interest when they do.

When you expose your vain imaginings to the light of God and His Word, and to a trusted person like your spouse, you rob them of their power. In the light, they cannot survive, and you bring them into submission to the Word of God.

So that is how you get ahold of your imaginings—by bringing them into the light. But the "vain" part is something else entirely. I have mentioned several times that pride and anger are connected, and pride and vanity are very connected. In fact, they can often be used interchangeably in different places in the Bible. In the next chapter, we're going to look at the connection between vain pride and anger, and I think what we discover may surprise you.

13
PRIDE: THE PRECURSOR TO ANGER

We have talked about tools for handling your anger, and we have talked about why we are angry as individuals and groups. However, now I want to look at our anger at a deeper level—at what causes anger.

At various points in this book, I have mentioned pride and anger together. Many people do not immediately connect these two, and I want to bring up the link between them now that you understand the danger of vain imaginations because pride is very dangerous to the angry person. It is both a cause of anger and will keep you from taking the action steps necessary to deal with your anger.

If you choose to stay in pride, you will often choose to stay in anger, and they both give the devil access to your life.

The world has a different view of the word "pride" than we do in the Church. They think this word is synonymous with taking pleasure in something done well or with self-esteem or self-confidence. However, this is not the biblical concept of pride. Some think that pride is simply thinking of yourself as better than others, and this is one component, but it is not typically the primary aspect of pride that contributes to anger.

Pride is the opposite of humility. Pride is putting yourself at the center and making it all about *you*. It is egotism, vainglory, or vanity—self-centeredness. When we are full of pride, we think our way is the only or best way, and when we do not get our way, we get angry. When it doesn't turn out the way we want it to, we get mad.

You know you have pride if you are always singing your own praises. If you are always critical of how others do things, you are dealing with pride. Do you have trouble apologizing or admitting your mistakes? Are you arrogant? Do you have trouble accepting feedback from others? These are all signs of pride.

Pride sets us up for disappointment, frustration, and anger. Pride sets us up to be angry because if you live long enough, you will see many things *not* go your way. They will not turn out the way you want, and then you are going to react.

Hurt, disappointment, offence, and anger are the fruit of pride.

When you do not humble yourself to accept that not everything can—or even should—turn out the way you want, you are founding a root of pride and bitterness that will lead to ongoing frustrated anger at others, at life, and at God.

Not everyone is going to treat you the way you want to be treated. Not everyone is going to do what you want them to. Not everything is going to go the way you plan, expect, or feel is fair. Bad things happen to good people, and good things to bad people. Plans go wrong, and unexpected and uncontrollable events can swoop in to change everything. God does not do everything the way we want Him to or in the timing we want Him to do it, and it is the height of pride to think that we know better than the Lord of lords and King of kings.

When we are in pride, we are saying that our way is *the* way—the *only* way. When this is between human beings, we can argue that our way is somehow better, but this is not always correct, and others will frustrate and even oppose us. When it is between us and God, our pride is us saying that we know better than He does.

Pride in this setting will pit us against God, and more significantly, God *against* us.

James 4:6 says, *"But He gives more grace. Therefore He says: 'God resists the proud, but gives grace to the humble.'"* Another translation says He *opposes* the proud. Think about that—being opposed by God. That means that you were on His team but got prideful and switched sides, and He is now *against* you! That is the level of frustration you are setting yourself up for with pride.

We must be willing to take the low road, to recognize it is not all about us, and to think of others first instead of ourselves (see Philippians 2:3). That means that we get out of the way, make it about them, not us, and let God be God. When we let go of pride like this and humble ourselves, we can accept what happens with faith, not anger, and we can look expectantly to God.

Pride is a blessing blocker. It blocks grace and your access to the power of God. It traps you in your arrogance, and it will prevent you from repenting and apologizing to others and to God, locking you into mistakes. It prevents you from taking the very action that will set you free. Pride will keep you in anger, struggling vainly against God to get your own way and hurting yourself in the process.

If there was a brick wall in the way and someone willfully crashed into it over and over, injuring himself trying to get through, would you blame the wall for being hard or the person for being hard-headed? If you are prideful and God is opposing you instead of giving you grace, you can crash against Him all you want, but the only one who's going to get injured is *you*. And it won't be God's fault.

Fear Begets Pride

Fear often lies under the surface of pride and anger. If we admit that we're wrong, we're afraid of the ways others will see us. We're afraid of being seen as a failure, or that admitting it somehow solidifies a mistake into being more real or more permanent than if we deny it. This is the truth behind why many people stick to their vain imagining instead of accepting the truth; we feel being wrong makes us look bad. We'd rather be wrong and keep our pride intact.

The truth of the matter is that if you have already messed up, you have already embarrassed yourself. You aren't saving any kind of face by denying it. It has already happened. You are deceiving yourself if you think that not admitting it somehow will make it like it never happened or make it go away. The path of integrity leads forward, not in denial of the past, and it looks like apologizing and making it right. There is no room for pride or anger in that process.

This is true of our interactions among people, and it is true of our interactions with God. When we mess up, we can either humble ourselves, take responsibility, repent, and turn away from our sin; or we can be prideful, pretend it never happened or that we're right, and put ourselves in opposition to God. Fear and pride will keep you from getting right with others and with God, and it will keep you stuck in your mess.

If you want to be free of anger, you must renounce your pride. You must determine that your way isn't the only way and acknowledge that God's way *is*. You must humble yourself and repent of your mistake and your pride.

I urge you to do this right now. Ask God to search your heart and expose to you any wicked way that He needs to correct. Take a deep breath and ask God to forgive you—not just for your mistakes, but for the pride that has kept you from saying you are sorry, repenting, and turning away from those wrong actions. Then, ask Him for healing for the fear that lies under the surface.

Turning away from pride looks much like the forgiveness process you have been learning in this book. We admit that we've made a mistake by being prideful, ask God for forgiveness, apologize to whomever we need to, and then turn away with our actions.

False Humility

The longer you've been saved, the more you must look out for false humility. The best example of this may be the elder brother in the story of the prodigal son, which I've mentioned before. When the prodigal comes back and the father throws a feast, the elder brother is angry and offended and will not go in. He tells the father all about how holy he is—how good he's been. He says he has always done what the father wanted, but all that time he'd never killed a fatted calf for him or thrown him a party, as he was for the prodigal, who'd messed up so completely.

The elder brother had great pride in his humility—in how good he'd been. But despite this supposed goodness, he did not understand the heart of his father, and his pride prevented him from going into the party and welcoming his brother with an open heart like the father had.

The elder brother let his pride keep him out of the blessing, and this is exactly what happens when we are prideful. This is an especially sinister problem in Church circles, because we can easily con ourselves into thinking we are humble when in fact we are religious and prideful. We can make it out about our performance—how good we are—and not about our heart.

How long have you been saved? How long have you been in church? The longer you have been, the more strongly I urge you to examine your heart right now. Together with the Holy Spirit, look very carefully at your life to make sure that pride and vanity are not in disguise as false righteousness and humility.

True Humility

The Father's heart is one of humility. Jesus did everything He saw the Father do, so whatever Jesus was like on earth, it was a reflection of the Father in Heaven. Jesus modeled humility to us.

Perhaps no other scripture explains Jesus' example of humility like Philippians 2:3-8, which says,

> *Do nothing out of selfish ambition or vain conceit. Rather, in humility value others above yourselves, not looking to your own interests but each of you to the interests of the others. In your relationships with one another, have the same mindset as Christ Jesus: Who, being in very nature God, did not consider equality with God something to be used to his own advantage; rather, he made himself nothing by taking the very nature of a servant, being made in human likeness. And being found in appearance as a man, he humbled himself by becoming obedient to death—even death on a cross!* (NIV 2015).

Humility is elevating the will of God above your own. It is committing to see His will done, thinking not of yourself but seeking only of seeing God's will done here on earth, as it is in Heaven.

Pride is putting you at the center. Humility is putting God at the center.

Your will and emotions are not going to like no longer being the center of your universe. Do you think Jesus wanted to go to the cross? He anguished over it so much, He sweat drops of blood! He cried out to God in prayer repeatedly, searching the face of the Father for an alternative. But in the end, He said, *"Father, if it is Your will, take this cup away from Me; nevertheless not My will, but Yours, be done"* (Luke 22:42).

If your emotions are in the driver's seat of your life—anger, selfishness, or anything else—you will not be able to humble yourself and submit to God's will. Our emotions must be submitted to the higher authority of the Word and will of God. You must have your spirit firmly buckled in behind the wheel, because in life there will always be "nevertheless" moments where our will is opposed to God's; and we must humble ourselves, as Jesus did, and submit to God's will.

And I will tell you this: You will often not understand what God is doing. We see now only in part and know in part, and if you are full of pride, that will make you angry. You will want it your way—the way you understand. Leaving it to God's way will seem frustrating, and if you let it, it will drive you to anger and bitterness with God.

We get frustrated when we don't understand things. It is natural. It is also natural to be frustrated when we do not get our way. There are times, even when putting God's will first, you will get frustrated. However, I am talking about taking that natural response and submitting it to God, then actively choosing His will *anyway*.

For instance, we all get angry from time to time. But if your anger is a lifestyle, and if you have become frustrated and angry with God because you do not understand His will and will not submit to it, your anger and pride will give the enemy a foothold. And that will lead you to a bitter root of chronic anger and being in opposition with God. An attitude like Christ's, one of humility, submits our will to God's.

Remember that forgiveness and thankfulness are choices, not feelings. Similarly, faith is not an emotion. We *choose* to have faith in Him no matter what comes our way, even when it is not what we want.

Just as forgiveness sets you free and thankfulness defuses anger, humility is the antidote to pride in your life.

It Is Not About You

At the core of humility is embracing that *it is not about you.* Humility is your willingness to submit to the will and Word of God. It is taking yourself out of the center of everything and placing Him there instead. When you don't let yourself become the center and submit yourself to God, you can stay in humility no matter what happens.

When you are full of pride, if God blesses you, you think it is about you. If you get money or see it as the reward, you will do things—even godly things—just to get the reward. If you think the blessing of God is about *your actions*, you are getting the blessing of the Lord out of its proper place. However, if you see the blessing He gives as a by-product of being humble, no blessing will negatively affect you, because you will stay humble.

Humility keeps things in their proper place—with God in the center. Your humility is not connected to how much you possess or do not possess. It is not the domain of the poor (or rich). The blessing from humility is directly connected to Whom you serve!

Do not get confused: Humility is not the same as timidity. In fact, a spirit of fear and timidity is actually another type of pride, because pride puts you at the center. Fear and timidity are just the flip side to arrogant, boastful pride; they are two sides of the same coin. They both can keep you from obeying God—one because you are too afraid, the other because you want it your own way.

"For God has not given us a spirit of fear and timidity, but of power, love, and self-discipline" (2 Timothy 1:7 NLT). You have upon you a spirit of power. It is not your own power, and you cannot change yourself or anyone else on your own power. You can, however, live in *God's* power by walking in godly boldness tempered by humility.

The most godly, powerful (again, not their power) people I have ever met are also the most humble. But they are not shy or humble—they are bold for the Lord! Because they know it is not about them; it is about Him.

Angry with God

However, it can sometimes be very difficult to act in humility when something happens in our lives that seems to be God's fault. We can find ourselves angry with God because we feel God had something to do with our problem—either letting it happen to us, or worse, causing it.

For countless years people have said thoughtless comments such as calling a catastrophe an "act of God" or saying, "God took him" when someone dies. When we pray and do not receive the answer that we want in the timing we want, when people get hurt or die, when bad things happen to good people, and other times things get difficult, we can be tempted to buy into the first lie—that God is not all good.

"God," we can find ourselves praying, "how could You let this happen?" Or, "Why are You doing this to me?" Perhaps you've asked, "God, why didn't You protect me?"

We can get hurt, disappointed, offended, and angry with *God* because we feel He let us down, was inattentive, or even was being mean or evil by causing something bad to happen to us. The hurts and disappointments are real, but the problem is they come from incorrect perceptions about God and what He does and does not do and what He does and does not promise. Let's finish this chapter up by dealing with this difficult problem together, because I think that God has shown me some things that will bring you peace.

First of all, if you find that you are angry with God, He is not going to hurl a lightning bolt from Heaven if you admit it. In fact, He already knows. He knew a long time ago! You admitting it is not news to Him, but it can be very helpful to you. Remember what I've said about lies—they lose their power in the open light of truth. If you are angry with God, the first step is simply admitting it to Him and to yourself.

Even before you feel it, practice forgiveness (He doesn't need our forgiveness, but we need to forgive because our feeling of pain is real). Choose to forgive, even if you are still hurting inside. Remember, when you forgive, you are setting free a prisoner—yourself.

Now, apologize—to God. Repent for blaming Him. Throughout the Word, which is truth, we read over and over that God is good. Jesus said it repeatedly, and the Psalms are filled with proclamations about His goodness. In fact, He is the only One who is good, and without Him there *is* no goodness! Whatever pain you are experiencing, *it is not God's fault.* You may feel like it is and need healing for that hurt, but God is assuredly not the author of anything bad or evil. His thoughts and actions to you are always for good, never to harm you, and He works things together for our good (see Jeremiah 29:11 and Romans 8:28).

That doesn't mean this always *feels* true. But if you have learned anything in this book it is that your feelings cannot be in the driver's seat of your life. Your spirit has received the truth of the Word, and the Word tells us that God is good—all the time, every time. If you are angry with God, after you acknowledge it and choose to forgive, it is time to repent and choose to take a different path.

If you are wrestling with anger against God, I challenge you to read the book of Job. Job, a righteous man, was not able to see the events going on in the spirit realm, and he questions God—and receives a powerful answer from the Lord. God's answer to Him is utterly and completely humbling. Force yourself to read it while praying for an open heart, and see the way the book ends.

As you consider that, contemplate this: We know Jesus said this of Himself: "*The thief does not come except to steal, and to kill, and to destroy. I have come that they may have life, and that they may have it more abundantly*" (John 10:10). If anything is being stolen, killed, or destroyed in your life, God is not behind it. The thief is!

There is a real thief, and his name is Satan. He is our enemy, and in him is *nothing* good. Yet throughout history, starting with Adam and Eve, he has been convincing us that God is the One who cannot be trusted! He, the father of lies, has tried to cast God in a bad light from the beginning, and he likes nothing more than getting us to be at odds with the only One who is good through pride.

Remember, if it is opposed to the truth of the Word, it is pride for us to believe it. If we are angry with God, that is pride, because it is directly opposed to what God says of Himself and the truth of the Bible.

You're Going to Need God Later

I do not have specific answers for you about why you lost a loved one, a job, or a child. I cannot tell you why you have gone through cancer or another health challenge, or why you have lost your joy. Job likely did not see into Heaven to see the exchange between God and the devil. But I can tell you this: If there is lying, stealing, killing, or destroying going on in your life, the fault lies with the accuser of the brethren, not the Lord Almighty.

It is time to surrender your pride, dear reader, and repent of it. God is a big God; He understands our human frailty (see Psalm 103:14). You can come to Him in lament (David did this often) and cry and wail to Him. I am reminded of a movie I once saw where a couple's daughter died. The wife came to the husband and cried and wailed and even pounded on his chest in her grief, and he did not fight her. He simply let her cry and go through her emotions, even the anger. Anger is a natural part of grieving a loss or hurt, and even if it is directed at Him, God loves you through it.

But you do yourself a great disservice by staying there. God is not our servant. He does not exist to give us what we want when we want it. If you wanted it your way, didn't get it, and now you are angry with God, you are pitting yourself against Him. If you remain angry with God, you are walking in pride, and it is time to let that go and turn away.

Don't box God in. Don't reduce Him to your magic genie. He is too big for us to fully understand, and His ways are as much higher than ours as the heavens are above the earth (see Isaiah 55:9). In this life, we will only see and know in part, not the whole, so you have a decision to make. You either choose to trust that somehow, some way, God's Word is true and He is good. Or you choose to believe the devil, buy into his lie, and put yourself at odds with the Creator of the Universe through your pride.

Dear reader, do not overlook this. Do not be in denial on this. If you are angry with God, own up to it. Forgive, repent, and get right with Him. It is your choice, and even if it requires that you choose every day to forgive, repent, and get right for you to deal with underlying anger toward God, it is worth it.

The practice of thankfulness is a powerful antidote for anger against God. If you will invest yourself in thanking God regularly, you will begin uprooting the anger against Him that has been poisoning your life. Humble yourself and praise Him; thank Him for everything He has done for you. Again, it is nearly impossible to be angry with someone—including God—when you are actively being thankful for them in prayer.

When you finish this chapter in a moment, sit down and write out why you are hurt, angry, and disappointed with God. Then, surrender that to Him in prayer. Let it go. Turn away from your pride, and choose to humble yourself before the Lord of lords and King of kings. He will restore the damage your pride and anger has done to your life, because He is quick to forgive and mighty to save! You do not want to stay angry with God, because you are going to need Him the rest of your life. It is not worth it to let *anything* come between you, and if you will work the tools I have given you, you can let go of your pride and anger toward God.

14

BLESSED ARE THE PEACEMAKERS

Earlier I said that God does not want us to stay angry, and I want to revisit something here at the end of the book. Sometimes we see things in the world that are not right, and it will make us angry. So, do we simply accept the bad things in this world as God's will? Is that pride, thinking that we know better than God?

No, and I will tell you how to judge this: When we see things that are wrong that do not line up with the will of God expressed in Scripture, it is righteous to be angered. David expressed this in the Psalms, frequently praying that his enemies, which were God's enemies, would be destroyed. We live under grace and do not pray for the destruction of our "enemies," but when we see injustice, sin, depravity, or other things directly opposed to God's character and His Word, it is right that it should anger us.

Now, we do not let this anger cause us to sin, but it can drive us to action. For instance, if a rough new bar opens near your neighborhood, attracting all kinds of unsavory-looking people, you can be angered by all the noise, or you can let it spur you on to praying for those people who need Jesus. In your anger, sin not; instead, witness to them. Love them. In this way, acting in line with the will of God is humility.

If you see someone on the news who was treated unjustly, you can let it make you angry. Or, you can let that urge you to pray for grace as the person gets through the situation, that change occurs in our country, and that our leaders become more aware of the problems. Perhaps it inspires you to organize an event at your church, to raise awareness among your friends and family, or to provide financial assistance to the abused person. If you just embrace your anger, you may find yourself burned up with frustration and becoming bitter.

I faced this recently when I planted some ferns on my property. We live on the corner, and I wanted these plants to provide some privacy because we couldn't build a fence. However, I unknowingly did not follow all the rules of the homeowners association. Well, it made one of my neighbors mad, because my bushes were too close to the curb.

I received a letter telling me to take down the bushes, and it was really my fault for not knowing and following the rules. However, what made me mad was that there were seven other homeowners who were also violating the rules, and the homeowners association was picking and choosing where they would enforce their rules by coming down on me and not them.

I did not like it, but I had to submit to the authority of the association and take out my bushes, and I could see the argument that if they grew they could hinder a driver's vision. But what really made me angry was the double standard. It was an injustice—a small one—but anger threatened to flare up in me. I had a choice to make.

At the beginning of this book, I told you that Jesus was once so angered by the state of the temple that He braided a cord into a whip and drove the money changers and those selling animals out of the temple. Zeal for His Father's house burned within Him (see Psalm 69:9)! But He didn't stay angry; He was moved with compassion. In fact, He allowed Himself to be killed by those very people.

Sometimes you may see something outside God's will like sickness, depression, abuse, or rebellion that will make you angry—not at the person, but at our enemy and the situation. Let it drive you to earnest prayer and godly action. When things are not according to God's will in our bodies, in our loved ones, and in our lives, that righteous anger should inspire us to pray and to act to see God's will done here on earth as it is in heaven.

I am motivated to teach God's truth when I see people misled or confused—it inspires me to preach. It makes me compassionate for people who don't know Christ. It urges me to reach out to them and share the love and grace that God has given to me. When I see people not living in the promises of God, not experiencing His blessing, I am compelled to teach them and mentor them and pray for them. Sometimes I'm angered by what I see the enemy has done to them, and it makes me want to teach them the truth and how to get victory in their situation.

Feeling angry is not a sin. It is a sin when we let it drive us to, in pride, violate God's Word, and if we do not deal with it in a godly way, it can give a foothold to the devil. But when it inspires us to respond in a godly fashion that brings God's will to earth, that can be a very good thing, and it can mirror the heart of our Father who is saddened and angered by the wages of sin on the earth.

I will tell you this clearly: You will not be able to respond to even righteous anger in a godly way if you are living in pride. It will color and distort what God wants to do, and it will bring your own will and emotions into the equation and rob that emotion of its godly direction, making it about you and what you want instead of about God and what He wants. It will cut off the opportunity and ruin the blessing you could be to others and yourself.

After my experience with my neighborhood homeowners association, I had a choice. I believe any kind of double standard is wrong, so I could either let this injustice make me angry or bitter, or I could choose to use the tools the Lord has given me and I have shared with you to deal with it.

I chose to buy popcorn for everyone on my cul-de-sac for Christmas. We tied big bows on each can of popcorn—good stuff from Chicago—and placed them on their porches Christmas Eve. This was the way God gave me to show His love to my neighbors, even though I really didn't like any of them. The Holy Spirit helped me get past my emotions in order to share the love He has poured into my heart.

Responding to righteous anger can only be done rightly in humility. It must be about bringing God's will to earth, not your own, and we must be transparent in the process. It must not be about us. When your will and emotions are submitted in humility to God, He can allow you to be angered by an injustice that's opposed to His Word and will use it to urge you on to love and good works, and when that happens, we can help bring God's will from Heaven to earth.

The Role of the Holy Spirit

I have repeatedly told you that you cannot change a lifestyle of anger on your own. Without God, we can only "manage" our anger. However, I want to emphasize again that *you are not alone!* The Lord sent you a Helper, the Holy Spirit (see John 14:16). He is the Spirit of Christ, and He is a Person and an equal part of the Trinity. Not to be feared, He is here for your benefit and to bless you with every spiritual blessing! And you *need* His fruit if you are to replace anger in your life.

He is the One who produces good fruit in our lives, and listen to the list of alternatives to anger that He provides: *"But the Holy Spirit produces this kind of fruit in our lives: love, joy, peace, patience, kindness, goodness, faithfulness, gentleness, and self-control. There is no law against these things!"* (Galatians 5:22-23 NLT) Don't those sound better than anger, frustration, rage, and bitterness? Don't they sound better than being out of control and then paying the consequences?

The Lord has poured His love into your heart through His Holy Spirit, and He is the One who provides the flow of peace. Earlier in the book, I shared with you a passage from Romans, and now I want to give you a little more context because it pertains to the promise of peace I want you to experience.

In Romans 5:1, Paul says, *"Therefore, having been justified by faith, we have peace with God through our Lord Jesus Christ."* Jesus made us right with God, and now the Holy Spirit pours love into our hearts. That way we can *"rejoice, too, when we run into problems and trials, for we know that they help us develop endurance. And endurance develops strength of character, and character strengthens our confident hope of salvation. And this hope will not lead to disappointment. For we know how dearly God loves us, because he has given us the Holy Spirit to fill our hearts with his love"* (Romans 5:3-5 NLT).

You would not be angry if everything had gone your way in life. You would not be frustrated if you'd gotten what you wanted, when you wanted it. You have experienced problems and trials, but now because of God's love and His peace and His blessing, instead of anger you can develop character and hope that will not disappoint. That way, when new troubles of any kind come, you can consider it an opportunity for joy, because you know that when you are tested, you have the chance to grow (see James 1:2-4).

This is made possible through the Holy Spirit. He has poured love into your heart so you can love others instead of being angry with them. He has poured out peace so that you can be a peacemaker.

The question is this: Will you let it out?

Will you let Him help you love those who make you angry? Will you let Him help you work for peace when you'd rather respond with anger?

Your emotions are not supposed to be in control. Your spirit is. Your spirit is led by His Spirit, and when you let the Holy Spirit lead you, you are acting like His children (see Romans 8:14). For me, that meant giving to my neighbors, even though I didn't like the decisions the homeowners association made. For you, it will be something different—but if you will listen, the Holy Spirit will speak to your heart and show you how to let your spirit lead.

The Promise of Peace

The promised benefit for dealing with your anger is not just "less anger." It has never been my desire that you simply "manage" your anger better in the style of this world. It is my prayer that, as you learn tools and make decisions, you are reaching toward a desired goal.

The goal is *peace*. My greatest desire for you is that you move from a place of anger to a place of peace, and I believe that the tools God had me share in this book are the keys that will help you attain the peace you seek in this life.

I do not use the word "peace" to mean that things are always bright and cheerful. Jesus tells us that in this world, we will have trouble (John 16:33), so we will never be completely trouble-free in this world. What I mean is that despite the things that may be going on, you can exchange anger and frustration for the kind of godly peace that will guard your heart and mind through Christ Jesus.

This is the peace that allows you to tackle life, even anger, without sinning. But God does not just want you to experience this peace in your own life; He wants you to be a peacemaker who brings peace to the earth.

Be a Peacemaker

Matthew 5:9 says, "*Blessed are the peacemakers, for they shall be called sons of God.*" Another translation says that God blesses those who *work* for peace.

Working for peace is the opposite of defaulting to anger. Being angry is easy; you just let your emotions be in charge and get ramped up when you do not like something. Choosing to *work for peace* involves using tools like the ones God showed me such as forgiveness and thankfulness. It takes effort to go against the flow, to go against your emotions. Your flesh wants you to embrace being frustrated and angry when you do not get your way.

But God has a different plan. His plan is that you may get angry, but you do not have to sin. His plan is that you do not *stay* angry, or live in anger. His plan is that you learn what to do with your anger. When you actively choose to use His tools to deal with your anger, you are choosing to be a peacemaker, and God will bless it. And when you become a peacemaker in your own life, the next step is to show others the peace God has given you so they will want it as well.

Psalm 133:1-2 says, "*Behold, how good and how pleasant it is for brethren to dwell together in unity! It is like the precious oil upon the head, running down on the beard, the beard of Aaron, running down on the edge of his garments.*" Imagine peace like a physical thing—like rich, soothing oil. In the Old Testament, oil poured over the head was both the literal symbol of the anointing, but also used medicinally. It represented the touch of God upon a selected leader, and it soothed and calmed hurts and abrasions.

Imagine how pleasant it would be for brethren within the Church to live in harmony and unity! Instead of anger, politics, and infighting within the walls of the Church, imagine churches full of unity— full of peace. Imagine the entire Body of Christ united in peace across the lines of denomination, doctrine, background, and race. Imagine the world seeing us in that peace and unity. What would unbelievers think if they saw us loving one another and acting in peace and unity? It would shake the world, because they would wonder what's wrong with us!

And they would want what we had.

We can begin that as individuals. How do we do this? We are the first to work for peace. We start in our own lives, and then we share what we've found with those around us.

The First to Make Peace

I have challenged you to take a step at various points in this book in order to tie action together with an idea or decision. I want to do that one more time. Decide right now that the next time you become angry with someone that you are going to be the first to move toward peace. Be the first to work for resolution, setting aside your pride and your right to be offended and choosing instead to forgive and search for common ground. There is a blessing to be found for those who are peacemakers.

What would you rather be: the peacemaker, or the peace taker? Those who work toward peace create it in their lives and share it with those around them. Those who are driven by their flesh suck the peace out of a room when they enter. So, which do you want to be?

Being a peacemaker is one of the strongest weapons against anger I have ever encountered. If you want to be a peacemaker, you are going to have to deal with your own anger, so bringing peace to those around you requires that you first welcome the Lord's peace into your own life.

Peace and anger cannot coexist. When you have created an environment of peace in your life by welcoming the Holy Spirit and handling your anger God's way, anger has no room in your life. Peace drives out anger; it gives it nowhere to live. Peace protects your life against anger, and it is made possible because of the Holy Spirit.

Spirit in the Driver's Seat

Your anger has gotten you this far, for better or worse. Wherever you are in life, you know that if you continue to be driven by anger, it will be your undoing.

However, through the power of God, you have chosen to no longer let anger be in the driver's seat of your life. You have chosen to make a change, to practice forgiveness, to embrace a lifestyle of thankfulness, to learn from your mistakes, and to move on and leave this angry chapter of your life behind. The Lord gave me these tools and techniques I shared with you, and they have the power to help you place your spirit firmly in the driver's seat of your life.

Anger's day is done, and you have decided to return it where it belongs—in the backseat, subjected to God. You no longer need to experience bitterness, depression, regret, and loneliness caused by a spirit of anger; you have chosen life and to be led by the Spirit of God. Your new life of grace, peace, and blessing begins because of your choice and your actions, and as you work the Lord's tools I have shared with you, you will climb out of the dark valley where anger drove you. Revisit them as often as you need to, and work hand-in-hand with God, through prayer, until you too receive freedom in this area. Practice forgiveness as a lifestyle, and learn to be thankful no matter what. Ask the Holy Spirit for help, and let the love He has poured into your heart flow out.

Freedom is coming, friend. Blessing is coming. Peace is coming. As you get better, you will make those around you—your entire environment—better because you learned to walk in peace instead of anger.

You mad? Not anymore! Now you are blessed!

Author Contact

If you would like to contact Dr. Dimitri Bradley, find out more information, purchase books, or request him to speak, please contact:

City Church
4700 Oakleys Lane
Richmond, VA 23231
804.222.7926
www.rvacity.org

www.facebook.com/drdimitribradley
www.twitter.com/dimitribradley
www.instagram.com/drdimitribradley